GW01157627

Corpus Li

22/10

Also available from Continuum:

Lexicology: A Short Introduction
M A K Halliday and Colin Yallop

Corpus Linguistics: Readings in a Widening Discipline
Edited by Geoffrey Sampson and Diana McCarthy

Using Corpora in Discourse Analysis
Paul Baker

English Collocation Studies: The OSTI Report
John Sinclair, Susan Jones and Robert Daley
Edited by Ramesh Krishnamurthy, with an introduction by
Wolfgang Teubert

*Meaningful Texts: The Extraction Information from
Monolingual and Multilingual Corpora*
Edited by Geoff Barnbrook, Pernilla Danielsson and
Michaela Mahlberg

Forthcoming:

Corpus Semantics: An Introduction
Wolfgang Teubert and Anna Čermáková

Text, Discourse and Corpora
Michael Hoey, Michaela Mahlberg, Michael Stubbs and
Wolfgang Teubert
With an introduction by John Sinclair

Corpus Linguistics

A Short Introduction

Wolfgang Teubert and Anna Čermáková

continuum

Continuum

The Tower Building	80 Maiden Lane
11 York Road	Suite 704
London	New York
SE1 7NX	NY 10038

First published in 2004 as part of *Lexicology and Corpus Linguistics*.

This edition © Wolfgang Teubert and Anna Čermáková 2007
Reprinted 2008

British Library Cataloguing-in-Publication Data
A catalogue record for this book is available from the British Library.

ISBN: HB: 0-8264-9480-3
         PB: 0-8264-9481-1

Library of Congress Cataloguing-in-Publication Data
A catalogue record for this book is available from the Library of Congress.

Typeset by YHT Ltd, London
Printed and bound in Great Britain by Athenaeum Press, Gateshead, Tyne & Wear

Table of Contents

1 Language and corpus linguistics

Wolfgang Teubert

1.1 Are all languages the same?

'According to Chomsky, a visiting Martian scientist would surely conclude that aside from their mutually unintelligible vocabularies, Earthlings speak a single language' (Pinker, 1994, p. 232). Indeed, if we discount the meaning of words, sentences and texts, our natural languages share many characteristics. They are linear. Utterances have a beginning and end, and between beginning and end we find a string of sounds or of characters, perhaps ideographic as in Chinese, or alphabetical as in most European languages. This is, of course, also the case for sign languages. An utterance in a sign language is again a string, in this case of signs such as hand and finger movements and facial expressions.

Utterances differ from pictures. Utterances are one-dimensional, pictures are two-dimensional. Even if we

1

try to describe a picture, the description will be inherently one-dimensional. Linearity would also be a characteristic of the language of the visiting Martian scientist. All languages are systems for signifying content. Each utterance has a content. But the content is not the utterance. The utterance is a sequence of signs which represent the content, which stand in place of the content. The utterance 'a Martian scientist visits Earthlings' can be said to represent an image, a photograph or a mental image which is two- or even three-dimensional. But the utterance is always a one-dimensional string of signs. John Sinclair, one of the pioneers of corpus linguistics, is fond of repeating what he believes to be a quote of the grammarian E. O. Winter that 'grammar is needed because you cannot say everything at the same time'. This is certainly the reason why all natural languages need grammar, and perhaps also why these various grammars can be described if not in identical, then in very similar terms.

Is this what Noam Chomsky meant (Chomsky 1957)? Not quite. Chomsky argues that all humans share the same language faculty, an innate faculty that regulates the ways signs are to be organized so that they become utterances. This is what is called grammar. In Chomsky's view, the innate language faculty shapes the grammar. This is not to say that all languages share the same grammar, not even on a deeper level. Today, in his minimalist programme, Chomsky sees the language organ as an apparatus that gives limited options. Adjectives, for example, can precede the noun they modify, or they can follow it. But all languages have adjectives and nouns and several other parts of speech. They are universal, they are shared by all human languages. So, and this is the important point, the language faculty is contingent, i.e. it happens to be the way it is, but it could have been different (and the language faculty of Martians might be different). The philosophical problem connected with this stance is that its credibility depends on conceiving of a convincing language, a language that could exist but does not exist – a language that does not comply with the settings of the language organ but is otherwise, in functional terms, equivalent to existing natural languages.

Chomsky's views on universal grammar are found in his book *New Horizons in the Study of Language and Mind* (Chomsky 2000, pp. 7–15). Whether he has succeeded in presenting his case convincingly is a matter of contention. Geoffrey Sampson (1997) in *Educating Eve: The 'Language Instinct' Debate* shows that there is evidence to the contrary in respect of many of the language features that Chomsky and Pinker claim as universals.

Traditional linguistics has been good at describing how syntax, morphology and inflection work. There is a set of basic assumptions, most of which have been around since classical times and which are used for describing any language that linguists stumble across. These assumptions include the facts that there is an entity we call a sentence, another entity we call a clause, that there are subjects, objects and predicates, and that there are words. There are different kinds of words, so-called parts of speech (from Latin *partes orationis*), featuring prominently among them: nouns, adjectives, verbs and adverbs (the big four), and less prominently others, such as pronouns, determiners, prepositions, and depending on the language or the particular grammatical theory, a few more or many more. In a language such as English, a word can come in different forms. The noun *table*, for example, can be a singular form (*table*) or a plural (*tables*). In many European languages a finite verb can be characterized by the properties person and number (e.g. first-person singular as in English *I laughed*, or first-person plural as in we laughed), tense (e.g. past tense, present tense), mood (e.g. indicative, subjunctive) and voice (active, passive). Words can be combined to form larger units such as noun phrases, or verb phrases, or other kinds of phrases, and several phrases can be put together to form a clause, or even a sentence.

There are of course differences in the details of grammatical description and theory, and all these entities form sets with fuzzy edges. For instance, some English -*ing* forms are usually described as verb forms ('she was laughing'), others as nouns ('laughing uses quite a few muscles'). Different linguistic schools tend to define these entities in different ways, and they give them different names. For example, in the sentence 'I enjoyed the concert', many linguists would call *the concert* the object (of the verb *enjoy*); but a more general term such as 'complement' may also be used, while some linguists would differentiate various kinds of 'objects', distinguishing, for example, between the material goal of verbs like *hit* and *break* and the object of behavioural or attitudinal verbs like *enjoy* and *dislike*.

The basic entities and categories of grammar are nevertheless common ground for many linguists. Whatever a specific school of linguists may call them, they are to a large extent translatable into each other. Noam Chomsky also subscribes to them. They are used to describe not just English, or other Indo-European languages, but, in principle, all languages. Some languages may display features that others do not have: for example, many Australian Aboriginal languages have a dual category in contrast to the singular and the plural, to indicate that there are exactly two, or a pair of entities; compare Pitjantjatjara *ngayulu* 'I', *ngali* 'we two', *nganana* 'we three or more'. Some languages, like Indonesian, do not have categories of the verb such as tense and mood. But principally it is the same finite set of entities and properties that we use to describe any of the Earthlings' languages, and it wouldn't be surprising if we used them also for all the Martian dialects once we came across them.

Smaller entities can be combined to form larger entities. Syntactic rules tell us which combinations are grammatical, and which are not. For many linguists, the smallest syntactic entities are words. For some, the morpheme is the smallest unit. Morphemes are parts of words, the smallest linguistic elements to which we can assign a meaning or a function. The word form *singing* consists of two morphemes: *sing* and *-ing*. The morpheme *-ing* can occur in most other verbs, as well; we find it in certain syntactic constructions, e.g. after a certain set of verbs like *help, see, hear*: 'he heard her singing in the rain'. Because its occurrence may be said to be caused by syntax, some linguists take morphosyntax to be part of syntax, and for them, morphemes are part of syntax. But generally, if syntax is held to be something different from the rest of the lexicogrammatical systems, it is understood to describe how words can be assembled to form a grammatical sentence.

Seen in this light, words are the basic tissue of syntax. They make up the vocabulary, the lexicon of a language. Linguists, including Chomsky, agree that the lexicon is a more or less finite list of lexical entries. Each lexical entry consists of the word, an indication of the part of speech it belongs to, and the syntactic and semantic properties it has. The entry for *boy* would tell us that it is a noun, that it is countable (hence there is a plural *boys*), and that it fits, according to specifiable rules and constraints, into a slot (i.e. a terminal element of the syntactic structure of a given sentence), which asks for a word denoting a human being (such as the subject and the object position of the verb *love*). The sentence 'Big boys love intelligent girls' could be described as having the structure: adjective + noun + (transitive) verb + adjective + noun. Each noun and the verb exemplifies a slot into

5

which we can insert a suitable lexical element taken from the lexicon.

Entities, properties and rules: this is the stuff that, according to Chomsky, constitutes each language. Therefore Chomsky's claim about the similarity of languages is not totally implausible. Languages resemble each other because their phonology, syntax and morphology can be described in the same – or at least similar – terms. For mainstream linguists, languages are all more or less the same. They may follow different rules, but they are made up of the same entities and share many properties.

But does this mean that entities, property types and rule types are language universals? This is not a question to which there is an easy answer. When we describe language, what kind of a reality are we describing? There are sound sequences, or chains of alphabetic characters (or other kinds of characters in languages that have non-alphabetic writing systems), which we are accustomed to interpret (successfully) as language. Linguists cut these strings into little bits and pieces and assign various functions to them. Certain bits (say, in English those that can be preceded by a determiner, that can serve as heads of noun phrases or prepositional phrases, and that can be modified by an adjective phrase or a prepositional phrase) we call nouns. But does that mean that nouns are more than bundles of properties that we construe in our theory? In the sentence 'This is a fake diamond', is *fake* a noun or an adjective? Obviously it is modifying the indisputable noun *diamond*. In this sense, it shares the properties of adjectives. But usually adjectives are gradable (*big, bigger, biggest; short, shorter, shortest*), whereas *fake* is not. And usually adjectives can be used predicatively, as in 'the house is big, but the garden is small', or 'isn't his hair short!' The word *fake* can occur predicatively ('this diamond is fake') but many people might prefer to say 'this diamond is a fake'. Grammatical description would seem to require that we say that *fake* is an adjective in 'this diamond is fake', but a noun in 'this diamond is a fake'. So it may be up to the linguist or the lexicographer to decide whether they describe *fake* as a noun that can be used as an adjective, or as an adjective that can be used as a noun. Observations like these should throw some doubt on the widespread belief that entities or categories such as nouns exist independently of their description, in the way that apples and pears would still exist, even as something categorically different, if there was no one trying to categorize them.

Linguistics, Chomsky tells us, should describe the human faculty of generating an unlimited number of different grammatical sentences. This is why he and many of his followers are opposed to an empirical study of language (where empirical means the analysis of existing texts). No amount of text, Chomsky claims, can account for the competence to distinguish non-grammatical structures from grammatical structures. If we accept the premise that we can always utter a (grammatical) sentence that has never been uttered before, then the criterion of grammaticality is not something that can be found in texts. Rather, it is a feature of our language faculty. It is the application of the rules that can generate endlessly new, never-heard-before, sentences, all of which are grammatical, because they comply with the rules. This competence to produce new grammatical sentences is something (ideal) native speakers have.

The language faculty is therefore a feature of the mind. If we want to find out how language works, we have to look at the mind, and not at texts. Let us, for a moment, return to the sentence 'Big boys love intelligent girls'. This sentence structure can demonstrate the generative power of the language faculty. We can say that this sentence structure consists of two parts, the noun phrase *big boys* and the verb phrase *love intelligent girls*. This verb phrase consists of a transitive verb (*love*) and another noun phrase (*intelligent girls*). Noun phrases must have a head, usually a noun (such as *boy* or *girl*), either in the singular or in the plural, which can be preceded by a determiner (*a* or *the*), and modified by an adjective (such as *big* or *intelligent*). Now, this structure can easily yield a seemingly endless amount of different sentences, by the insertion of other nouns and verbs into the respective slots ('little girls hate spiteful boys', 'intelligent women admire intelligent men', and so on). Some verbs may not go well with some nouns, as in: 'Fake diamonds hate eternity'. It seems we must therefore apply other rules as well that make sure that only those nouns are selected which go together with a particular verb. (For Chomsky, those so-called sub-categorization rules are part of syntax, not of semantics, a position that is arguable.)

Chomsky's revolution in linguistics is about the generative power of rules. Rules, he says, do not describe what is there but what is possible. This focus on the generative aspect of language has changed the agenda of linguistics. The role of linguistics is no longer to interpret what we find in existing texts, but to describe the language faculty, or, in abstract terms, the competence of a speaker to produce new grammatical sentences. While rules were once formulated by language experts in order to facilitate the understanding of existing texts, or to help us to learn a foreign language, the task for a Chomskyan linguist is to discover the rules we follow as native speakers without even being aware of them, i.e. the rules which constitute the language faculty of human beings. In traditional linguistics, entities or categories, like nouns, or tense, or person, were useful constructs in the framework of a theory. Rules were expressions of the linguist's ingenuity to make sense of the language evidence. Under the new agenda, language is like a game of chess. We are born with the capability to follow the rules without ever having to learn them. Chomskyan linguistics thus changes the status of linguistic rules. Rather than being tools for language analysis, they now become the metaphysically real essence of language.

Pre-modern linguistics in Europe was not concerned with the productivity of language. From the Middle Ages well into the nineteenth century, linguists were philologists, which was, at the time, more or less synonymous with classicists. Their research was on 'dead' languages: Latin, Greek and Hebrew. Their aim was not to produce new texts in these languages; they wanted to understand the texts we had inherited from ancient times. The rules they came up with were rules to help us make sense of the sentences. The rules were meant to describe what we were confronted with in the texts; they were not designed to empower us to become competent speakers of ancient Greek. The grammatical rules philologists were interested in were those that explained the specificity of Greek as compared to other languages, those that helped to understand their texts. Philologists were not interested in what was universal. Their rules were descriptive; they had to facilitate the analysis of textual evidence.

The philologists may not have had a scientific method. And yet we inherited from them the academic editions of classical and oriental texts we are still using today, together with comprehensive dictionaries, or rather glossaries, citing each noteworthy occurrence of any word embedded in its contexts and still providing an irreplaceable aid in understanding these texts.

Hermeneutics was the philosophical basis not of linguistics as we know it today but of philology. Hermeneutics is the art (or craft) of interpretation. In the early Middle Ages, this meant interpretation particularly of the Bible, but later also of the other classical texts. The goal of hermeneutics is to find out what a text means.

What, indeed, does a text mean? Do we have to find out what the authors *thought* was the meaning of their texts? The authors might not tell us that explicitly, or they might tell us but be deceiving us in one way or another. Whatever they say, it is not the meaning of their texts. Or is the meaning of a text what the text means to me? Then meaning is something subjective, individual, something that cannot be validated by other readers. Meaning must be something else. When we encounter the word *love* in a medieval text, can we find out what the word meant then? Is there a methodology to answer this question? Is there a possibility of coming to an understanding that is shared by our fellow linguists? This is the key question hermeneutics is concerned with.

Particularly in the English-speaking countries, hermeneutics and philology have lost much of their earlier appeal. Since the first years of the twentieth century, British empiricism has given way to the new paradigm of analytic philosophy. This brand of philosophy, dating back both to Cambridge and connected with names such as Bertrand Russell, and equally to the Vienna circle and connected with names such as Mach, Carnap and (the young) Wittgenstein, is concerned with truth and reality. The question that is at the core of the current mainstream paradigm of the philosophy of language is not what a text, a sentence, a word means but how we can know whether it is true, whether it truly reflects the discourse-external reality or not. This is not a question hermeneutics, or philology, is concerned with. Philologists do not want to know under which conditions the sentence 'Mary, the mother of Jesus, was a virgin' is true; they content themselves with the exploration of the meanings of words – for example, with questions such as whether the English word *virgin*, Latin *virgo*, Greek *parthenos* are appropriate translations of Hebrew *almah*, a word which usually just means 'young woman'.

Today, hermeneutics and philology are often considered dull, continental and old-fashioned. Edward Said, the famous Lebanese-American orientalist, is a noble exception. For him, philology is 'the extraordinarily rich and celebrated cultural position' that (not only) gave classics and orientalism their methodological basis. The philologist is the interpreter of bygone texts on the horizon of our own modernity. The philologist makes us understand cultural and intellectual history. This act of understanding is two-directional. Our understanding of these texts always also presents a challenge to the way in which we understand ourselves. Thus, 'philology problematises – itself, its practitioner, the present'. Said quotes Ernest Renan, a nineteenth-century orientalist: ' "The founders of the modern mind are philologists". And what is the modern mind ... if not "rationalism, criticism, liberalism [all of which] were founded on the same day as philology" ' (Said 1995, p. 132). What has made philology so unattractive in more recent years? Perhaps it is the sense of arbitrariness, of subjectivity, the lack of a truly scientific method. Interpreting a text is always an act, as opposed to a process that follows clearcut rules. The art of hermeneutics, the craft of philology always involves making decisions. It means choosing between alternatives, without unambiguous instructions on how to select one of the options.

In the nineteenth century we find a novel interest in languages, different from traditional philology. It was the century when the enlightenment finally bore fruit and nature began to be understood in terms of the laws of nature. The main foundations of the sciences as we know them today were laid. All the academic glamour now rested with the sciences; and the liberal arts, including the humanities, were relegated to backstage. The hermeneutical approach to language was not interested in immutable, eternal laws or rules. But that did not

11

necessarily mean that there weren't any. The first domain of this new 'scientific' approach to language was the study of relationships among languages. That became the starting point of modern linguistics. It seemed that many languages spoken in Europe, in the near East and even as far away as India, were somehow related to each other, some closer, like Gaelic and Breton as Celtic languages, Lithuanian, Latvian and Old Prussian as Baltic languages, or Czech, Polish and Russian as Slavonic languages. There was Sanskrit, there were the Romance languages, there were the Germanic languages and many more, dead or alive. They all seemed to descend from one single language, Indo-European, and in the course of history they seemed to have become more and more separated from each other. Over the course of their existence, all these languages underwent change. What was *patēr* in Greek and *pater* in Latin became *padre* in Italian, *père* in French, *Vater* in German and *vader* in Dutch. English *father* developed from Old English *fæder*. All of them share, ultimately, the same ancestor. Similarly we can work out that the English word *rich* is related to the German *reich*, that early Germanic took the ancestral form of these words from Celtic, and that they are also related to the Latin *rex*, 'king'; or that the English word *glamour* is borrowed from Scots, while, in turn, the Scots word is derived from English *grammar*, which is, in turn, taken from Latin *(ars) grammatica*.

To the linguists of the nineteenth century who studied these phenomena, it seemed that the phonetic changes these words underwent in the course of history were governed by laws. The new linguists were less concerned with interpreting the meanings of texts, sentences, or words; they wanted to discover the laws of phonetic change. They were so confident in their scientific powers that they did not shy away from reconstructing ancestral languages, like Indo-European, even though no texts had survived. For the first time, it had become possible to describe language in terms of rules; rules that did not involve any decision-making on the part of the linguists, rules that produced results that had to be objectively correct once you accepted the premises. And if there were laws in phonetic change, there must also be laws for grammar. Therefore we can find, from the middle of the nineteenth century, a surge of literature on grammar, coinciding with a relegation of linguistic literature dealing with the vocabulary and the meaning of words to a less prominent position. This is still the situation in which we find ourselves today.

The modern linguists who succeeded the philologists saw themselves as scientists. However, from Ferdinand de Saussure and the structuralists of the Prague school, to Louis Hjelmslev and Roman Jacobson, these linguists were not interested in the mental processes linked to language. They wanted to investigate the structure of language, based on analyses of texts, in order to understand the language system behind it, what Saussure called *la parole*. They wanted to describe a system of rules and means that existed independently of its individual speakers and its historical development (language synchrony) – although this system could also be studied from the historical point of view as a system gradually undergoing change according to language laws (language diachrony).

Thus the preoccupation with rules and laws characterizes both non-Chomskyan modern linguistics (henceforth: standard linguistics, preoccupied with the idea of the system) and the Chomskyan variety of language studies (less interested in the system). Both varieties look at language as a system, which can be described in terms of rules, entities, categories and properties. From the structural point of view, these laws, entities and properties are, on a general level, more or less identical for all human languages, though rather, and at times profoundly, different in particulars.

Yet while Chomsky insists on the fundamental sameness of all languages (on a biological level), he also points out something very important: the vocabularies of all these languages across the world are (mostly) mutually unintelligible. People do speak different languages, and we do not understand each other. Doesn't this contradict the claim of sameness? In general, Chomsky's interest in the lexicon is, contrary to structuralists, only marginal. But how important is the lexicon? How important is it to find out about the meanings of words?

1.2 Standard linguistics and word meaning

Even if Chomsky is technically wrong in positing an innate mechanism that determines, by a minimum of external input, the grammar of the language we grow up with, it still remains a fact that we seem to have much less difficulty in learning the syntax of a foreign language than its vocabulary. It is not always too difficult to construe grammatically correct sentences in a second language. But unless we are acquainted with it very thoroughly, we will make mistakes when we try to put our thoughts into words or to translate a text from our native language. We can follow rules easily. But how can we do the right thing if it seems all but impossible to teach us what is the right thing? This is indeed the impression if we attempt to let ourselves be guided by bilingual dictionaries. They offer many choices but few instructions.

The difference between grammar and vocabulary is largely a matter of perspective or method. For vocabulary, at least at first sight, there seem to be few rules which we can follow. Rules we can learn, and instructions we can follow. But no bilingual dictionary seems to be big enough to tell us how to translate an apparently quite simple word, like *grief*, into French. There are, according to the *Collins–Robert French Dictionary* (1998, repr. 2001), two main options: *chagrin* and *peine*. We are, however, not clearly told which of the alternatives to choose when. In the absence of clear instructions, even the most comprehensive bilingual dictionaries let us down when we want to translate a text into a non-native language.

The same dictionary gives us, as the equivalents for *sorrow*, the same two words it has given us for grief, *peine* and *chagrin*, plus another word, *douleur*, which is preceded by the ominous comment: '(stronger)'. It is not quite clear what this means: is this the word to use if your grief is stronger than average grief, or is *douleur* a stronger word than *peine* or *chagrin*? From the French perspective the two equivalents *sorrow* and *grief* appear to be synonyms. However, most native speakers of English agree that in these two sentences 'Grief gave way to a guilt that gnawed at him' and 'A magic harp music made its listeners forget sorrow', *grief* cannot be replaced by *sorrow*, and vice versa, so that, at least from the monolingual English perspective, they cannot be regarded as synonyms. Things get even more confused when we look up, in our bilingual dictionary, the English equivalents for the French word *chagrin*. For *chagrin* we find: '(= affliction) grief, sorrow', and thus we become curious what French *affliction* means in English. The only English equivalent we are offered, though, is *affliction*. The French equivalents of English affliction are *affliction* and *détresse*, while *détresse* is, we are told, *distress* in English. As the English equivalents of *peine* we find *sorrow* and *sadness*, but not *grief*. Our analysis thus reveals a distressing absence of systematicity, and we are left wondering whether this is due to the languages as they

15

are or due to our inability to describe them properly. (And it has to be said that the *Collins–Robert* is not just any French–English dictionary. Together with the *Oxford–Hachette French Dictionary*, it represents the apogee of modern bilingual lexicography.)

The meaning of words, as compared with the regularities of phonetic change and sentence construction, is generally fuzzy and vague, not only when we compare one language with another, but also from a monolingual perspective. Words, single words, may be the ideal core units when it comes to describing the working of grammar. But they are much less the appropriate core units when we are interested in meaning. Single words are commonly ambiguous. Dictionaries capture this ambiguity by assigning two or more word senses to a word. As shown above, we are confronted with the ambiguity of single words whenever we want to translate into a foreign language. Then we have to choose between several options, only one of which is acceptable. But when we read a sentence or text we are not fooled, under normal conditions, by any ambiguity. Usually we have no problem understanding what a sentence means. This is because we do not look at the words in isolation, but embedded in a context. We read a word together with the words to its left and to its right; we have no problem in knowing what a word means. Ambiguity is a consequence of our misguided belief that the single word is the unit of meaning. Units of meaning are, by definition, unambiguous; they have only one meaning. While some words are units of meaning, many are not.

This enquiry into meaning makes the case that meaning is an aspect of language and cannot be found outside of it. It is entirely within the confines of the discourse that we can find the answer to what a unit of meaning means, be it a single word or, more commonly, a collocation, i.e. the co-occurrence of two or more words.

A unit of meaning is a word (often called the node or keyword) plus all those words within its textual context that are needed to disambiguate this word, to make it monosemous. As most of the more frequent words are indeed polysemous, they do not, as single words, constitute units of meaning. As any larger dictionary tells us, for example, the word *fire* is ambiguous. It is therefore not a unit of meaning. In combination with the noun *enemy* it becomes a part of the collocation *enemy fire*, meaning 'the shooting of projectiles from weapons by the enemy in an armed conflict'. This collocation is (under normal circumstances) monosemous, and therefore a unit of meaning.

In the venerable field of phraseology, people have always been aware that language is full of units of meaning larger than the single word. When we hear 'She has not been letting the grass grow under her feet', we do not expect that to be literally true. Rather we have learned that the phrase 'not let the grass grow under one's feet' is an idiom, a unit of meaning which, according to the *New Oxford Dictionary of English* (2001) (*NODE*), means 'not delay in acting or taking an opportunity'. Indeed, the idiomaticity of language is a favourite topic of the discourse community. People like to talk about idioms; we feel that they are an important part of our cultural heritage. There is many a book explaining their origins, and there is hardly a dictionary that would dare to leave them out. Over the last century, we have come up with ever more refined typologies of idioms. Rosamund Moon's excellent study *Fixed Expressions and Idioms in English* (1998) provides a thorough corpus-based analysis of the phenomenon of idiomatic language. While some idioms are more or less inalterable ('it's raining cats and dogs'), others are somewhat ('a skeleton in the closet', 'a skeleton in the cupboard'). Most idioms oscillate between the two extremes of invariance and alterability. If we probe too deeply, our 'intuition' will often desert us. Are 'figments of imagination' an idiom, or can there be other figments? Does figment have a meaning of its own? We have to look in a corpus (here the British National Corpus) to find that there are indeed other figments, namely 'figments of linguistic bewitchment' and 'figments of fiction'. In the singular as well, there are some deviations from the prototypical collocate *imagination*: 'a figment of his own mind; a figment of my neurosis; a figment of its leaders' fantasies; a figment of his own name'. But these are four instances (i.e. less than 5 per cent) out of fifty-eight occurrences.

Idioms have found their way into bilingual diction-aries as well. The *Wildhagen Héraucourt German–English Dictionary* (1963–72) tells us that the English equivalent of *wie ein Blitz aus heiterem Himmel* [literally: like a bolt from a serene sky] is 'like a bolt from the blue'. Idioms feature rather prominently in foreign-language learning – with the result that speakers of English as a second language tend to overuse those they have learned, such as 'it's raining cats and dogs' (an idiom not greatly used by native speakers).

Modern linguistics has taught us that there is, indeed, a range of lexical constituents that can lay claim to being a unit of meaning. There are bound morphemes which have a meaning only by virtue of being part of a larger constituent (as the plural -*s* in English); there are free morphemes whose meanings seem to be rather invariable; there are words; and there are idioms, including proverbs, making up a full sentence. We have also learned that the borderlines between them are areas of contention. But while we would never doubt that morphemes are linguistic constructs, we have come to accept the ontological reality of the word.

Today, when we hear 'word', we normally think first of 'an element of speech', as the second sense given in the *OED* (1989) is circumscribed. If we believe Jack Goody

(Goody 2000), this concept is foreign to oral societies. That is not so astonishing. In spoken language we normally do not insert a pause between words. Neither were the Greeks and Romans of antiquity in the habit of putting spaces between their written words. Where the space is inserted is largely a matter of convention, and not always well-established convention. Look in any large English dictionary for entries beginning with *half*. One dictionary has *half brother* as two words, another gives it a hyphen: *half-brother*. One has *halfback* as a single word, another has it with a hyphen. And so on. What is *linguistique de corpus* in French is *corpus linguistics* in English and *Korpuslinguistik* in German. There is no cogent reason other than tradition why there should be no space between the elements of German compounds, i.e why it is *Korpuslinguistik* rather than *Korpus Linguistik*.

Other modern languages missed the chance to define words by spaces. When it was recognized that in most cases it did not make sense to define a single Chinese character as a word and it became accepted that most Chinese words would consist of two or even three characters, it became a problem to identify words in a sentence. It is often the case that Chinese sentences can be cut up into words in different ways as long as we apply nothing but formal rules and leave out what they mean. Thus, in Chinese-language processing, there is still no segmentation software that is entirely reliable. How could it be different? We find cases of doubt in practically all Western languages. The problem of where there should be spaces and where not featured prominently in the German spelling reforms introduced in the mid-1990s.

Listening to foreign languages which we do not understand makes us even more aware of this problem. How do we know where a word begins and where it ends? Normally, people do not mark word boundaries phonetically. How do we know if two occurrences of the same concatenation of phonemes are occurrences of the same word (e.g. *no* versus *know*)? How can someone who does not speak English find out that *a* and *an* are two variants of the same word, the indefinite article, or that *the* in *the enemy* and *the* in *the friend* are variants of the same definite article, even though they are usually pronounced differently?

Languages in written form seem, at first, to simplify matters for us, particularly if they are written in the Latin alphabet. There we find spaces between the words. But how reliable are they? We have already seen some variation with words beginning with *half*. Is *half time* the same as *halftime* and *half-time*? Some dictionaries distinguish the musical term *half tone* from the printing term *halftone*. If *corpus linguistics* is one word in German (*Korpuslinguistik*), why is it two words in English? Or is it not? Do compounds consist of two words, or are they, in spite of the space between the two elements they consist of, just one word? Are words in languages such as Hungarian or Welsh, which often seem to consist of a rather large number of elements, words in the same sense as English words? One Finnish word *talossanikin* means 'also in my house', which is translated as four words in English. In Chinese, we find the same spaces between all characters and there is no special indicator telling us which characters belong together or where a word begins or where it ends. In order to identify words we have to rely on wordlists and dictionaries. But they are the more or less arbitrary results of lexicographers at work. What are we left with once we take away the spaces between words?

We have always known that there are units of meaning larger than the single word. From early childhood, we are made aware of them. A phrase like 'to turn a blind eye to something' has become part of our cultural heritage. It is an idiom, and idioms have always been listed in our dictionaries. Yet we are not so readily aware that large portions of our texts are also made up from larger, often rather complex units of meaning, like *weapons of mass destruction* or *friendly fire*. For the most part, these are absent from our dictionaries. With our ingrained focus on the single word, that is not surprising. The larger units escape the attention of even experienced and well-trained lexicographers. They do not catch the eye when we come across them. Before the advent of corpora and of corpus linguistics, we did not even have a methodology to detect them. Neither standard linguistics nor Chomskyan linguistics can identify these units of meaning.

What is it then that makes the single word continue to be such an attractive unit in linguistics? Words seem to be almost ideal units for grammars, particularly grammars that do not touch on meaning. Noam Chomsky's *Syntactic Structures* (1957) is a good example. Here we find sentences (S), non-terminal symbols such as noun phrases (NP) and verb phrases (VP), and terminal symbols such as nouns (N), adjectives (Adj), determiners (Det), verbs (V), etc. Grammatical rules, starting with the S-symbol, generate strings of terminal symbols. In principle, we can insert the corresponding lexical elements in the slots provided by these symbols. Those lexical elements are single words. Up to a point, such a grammar seems to work, particularly for non-inflecting languages with a strict word order. We run into real trouble only when we demand that the sentences generated by this grammar make sense, that the sentences can be interpreted semantically. For a meaning-free grammar, the single word seems to be indeed the lexical element *par excellence*. In language learning, meaning-free grammars are good enough for constructing grammatical sentences in the target language, regardless of what they mean.

21

It is meaning, not grammar, that casts a shadow over the single word. A glance at any monolingual or bilingual dictionary confirms that the main problem of single words, from a semantic perspective, is their polysemy, their ambiguity and their fuzziness. For the verb *strike*, the *NODE* lists 11 senses. One of them is 'make (a coin or medal) by stamping metal'. As a sub-sense of this we find 'reach, achieve, or agree to (something involving agreement, balance, or compromise): the team has struck a deal with a sports marketing agency'. Though we might, upon consideration, come to accept this sense as a metaphorization of striking coins, the actions seem to have hardly anything in common. The *strike* in *strike a deal* means something other than the *strike* in *strike coins*, and something different from the other ten senses ascribed to it in the dictionary entry. Indeed one could easily maintain that it has no meaning of its own; together with *deal* it does mean something, namely 'reach an agreement'. This is the gist of John Sinclair's article (1996) 'The empty lexicon'. Once we have identified semantically relevant collocates of words like *strike* (*a blow*, *a deal*, *oil*, etc.), their ambiguity and fuzziness disappears. The collocation *strike a deal* is as monosemous or unambiguous as anyone could wish. Even though neither the *NODE* nor the *Longman Dictionary of English Idioms* (1979) lists *strike a deal* as an idiom, it seems to belong in this category. In the British National Corpus (BNC) there are 25 occurrences of *struck a deal*. The absence of *strike a deal* from larger dictionaries and specialized idiom dictionaries illustrates that the recognized lists of idioms, those we are aware of as part of our cultural heritage, represent no more than the tip of an iceberg. Time and again, corpus evidence suggests that there are many more semantically relevant collocations than dictionaries tell us.

What about the sense of *strike* described in the

NODE as 'discover (gold, minerals, or oil) by drilling or mining'? In the Bank of English, there are 23,096 occurrences of *struck*. In a random sample of 500 occurrences, we find 7 instances for this sense of *strike*, 4 of 'struck gold', 2 of 'struck oil', and 1 of 'struck paydirt'. All of these citations represent metaphorical usage. Here are two examples:

> Dixon, who, together with the unfailing Papa San, struck gold with 'Run The Route'.

> telephone franchises. No one has struck paydirt yet, although the Bells have captured business

The example of *strike* 'discover by drilling or mining' shows that there is no obvious feature to tell us whether we should analyse a phrase as consisting of two separate lexical items (*strike* and *gold*) or whether we should analyse it as a collocation, i.e. as one lexical item (*strike gold*). It is not a question of ontological reality, of what there is, but a question of expediency. Carrying things to extremes and replacing most single words in our dictionaries by collocations would mean that these dictionaries would have to become much more voluminous. We would have to account for *strike a chord*, *strike a balance*, *strike a blow*, *strike a pose*, *strike a note*, *strike fear*, *strike terror*, *strike home*, *strike someone (as)* and possibly some others. If we leave things as they are, we find *strike a coin* and *strike a deal* belonging to the same sense category. Expediency alone, however, seems to be unsatisfactory. Aren't there any more plausible arguments?

1.3 Words, idioms and collocations

Let us look at another example in more detail. Some grammatical patterns are particularly prone to form collocations, such as nouns modified by adjectives. This fact has not escaped the attention of lexicographers. However,

23

without the application of the methodology developed for corpus linguistics, it seems to be left to the whims of dictionary-makers what they decide to include. For the adjective *false*, the *American Heritage Dictionary* (4th edition, 2000) lists these collocations: *false alarm, f. arrest, f. consciousness, f. fruit, f. imprisonment, f. indigo, f. ipecac, f. memory syndrome, f. miterwort, f. pregnancy, f. pretense, f. rib, f. Solomon's seal, f. spikenard, f. start.* The *NODE* lists these collocations: *false acacia, f. alarm, f. bedding, f. card, f. colour, f. coral snake, f. cypress, f. dawn, f. economy, f. face, f. friend, f. fruit, f. gharial, f. helleborine, f. memory, f. move, f. oxlip, f. pretences, f. rib, f. scorpion, f. start, f. step, f. sunbird, f. teeth, f. topaz, f. vampire.* Even if we acknowledge the differences between American and British English, there are surprisingly few overlaps: *f. alarm, f. fruit, f. memory, f. pretense/pretences, f. rib, f. start.* A random sample of 50 citations from the BNC attests *false alarm, f. dawn, f. pretences, f. start, f. teeth,* but in addition many other collocates of *false: assumptions, cheerings, claims, complaints, confidence, declarations, decisions, denial, distinctions, echo, enquiries, expectations, formastation* (!), *hopes, idea, information, market, money, position, proportion, readings, reasoning, report, take, testimony, theory, tradition, understanding, witness.* Which of these co-occurrences should be described as two separate lexical items, which as a single lexical item? How many senses should we ascribe to *false*? Does *false* in *false alarm* mean something different from *false* in *false echo* or *false witness*? Or would it make things easier to say that it does not really matter what *false* means in these instances and we should rather try to describe what *false alarm, false echo* and *false witness* mean? Which cases should we describe as collocations, which as a combination of (one meaning of) *false* with (one meaning of) the noun in question?

Within the confines of one language it is impossible to come up with clear criteria. But once we bring in a second language, we suddenly find the arguments we have been looking for. The *Wildhagen–Héraucourt* dictionary tells us that these are all possible German equivalents of *false*: 1. *falsch, unrichtig, irrig; ungesetzlich, widerrechtlich*; 2. *unwahr; trügerisch, täuschend; verräterisch, treulos; untreu*; 3. *falsch, gefälscht; unecht; nachgemacht; vorgetäuscht; blind; vorgeblich; Falsch-, Schein-; irrig, so genannt.* How helpful is such an entry? The senses are being distinguished by the different sets of equivalents. But some of the equivalents occur in more than one set. Does that mean that the equivalents themselves are polysemous, or just that the sense categories are fuzzy? (Note that *falsch* is the first and, implicitly, most significant equivalent for both sense 1 and sense 3!) For those who know some German it is also immediately obvious that the words we find within a given sense are far from synonymous; we cannot simply substitute them for each other in various contexts. Why then are we given three senses, and not one, or maybe ten or twenty? If we speak German well, the list of words will help us to choose the one that fits best into a given context. If we do not know German that well, how are we to choose the appropriate equivalent?

Naturally, the lexicographers are aware of their predicament. If they want to cater to native-English speakers with a cursory knowledge of German they have to deliver more. They have to give the translation equivalents not of *false* but of *false* in combination with the nouns it co-occurs with. They have to provide the translations for the collocations of *false*. Some of these collocations are listed as additional information within a given sense category. For sense 1 we find: *false quantity, false arrest, false imprisonment.* For sense 2 we find: *false mirror, false oath* [the equivalent given is *Meineid*], *false pretences, false swearing.* For sense 3 we find *false coin, teeth, hair*; and the idiom *to sail under false colours*. There is also a subsequent section called *Verbindungen* ['collocations'] with more phrases: *false alarm, f. bottom, f. cap, f. door, f. key, f. ogive, f. shame, f. report, f. step, f. take-off.*

Looking at the *Oxford–Duden* (compiled 1990, i.e. *c.* 50 years after the first edition of the *Wildhagen*), *false* is again divided up into three senses. Again slightly abridged, sense 1 is *falsch; Fehl- (Fehldeutung, ...); Falsch- (Falschmeldung, ...); treulos; gefälscht;* sense 2: (*sham*) *falsch; künstlich; geheuchelt; gekünstelt;* sense 3: (deceptive) *falsch; unberechtigt; trügerisch.* There is no way to map these three senses on to the three senses of the *Wildhagen–Héraucourt.* The users are left in doubt whether the division into senses in either of the dictionaries reflects the way *false* is being used in English or the hypothesis that there are three different main translation equivalents of *false* in German. Neither claim seems to be particularly helpful or supported by evidence. It just happens that *COBUILD* (the *Collins COBUILD English Language Dictionary,* 1987) also divides *false* up into three senses, identified as (1) 'incorrect', (2) 'artificial' and (3) 'insincere'. The *Oxford–Duden treulos* (sense 1), however, does not sail under 'incorrect'; neither does *geheuchelt* (sense 2) travel under 'artificial', nor *unberechtigt* (sense 3) under 'insincere'. As to German ways of negotiating word meanings, it would be next to impossible to claim that *treulos* and *gefälscht* belong to the same category, or *künstlich* and *geheuchelt*, or *unberechtigt* and *trügerisch.*

However, this dictionary entry could give us some ideas on how to be more helpful to its users. For translating into our own native language we might welcome a list of all relevant equivalents (in order of frequency or alphabetic order) so that we might choose among them on the basis of our linguistic competence. For translating into a language other than our own, a language where we do not have a comparable competence, we would, first of all, need a default translation. In the case of *false*, that is easy. According to the *Oxford–Duden*, the first equivalent in each of the three sense categories is *falsch*. This is no doubt the most common equivalent, being closely related to it etymologically. This translation equivalent should be used whenever *false* is not followed by a noun that is given in a subsequent list of collocations. In bilingual lexicography, we can define a collocation as a phrase that cannot be translated using the default translations offered for its components. Thus, users do not need to be told that the equivalent of *false teeth* is *falsche Zähne*, because that would be the default translation anyway. (Actually the Germans more commonly use *Gebiss*, a word used more often than *dentures* is in English.) But they do need to know that the equivalent of *false coin* is *Falschmünze* (as opposed to *falsche Münze*). How do we arrive at such a list of collocations? If we compare the lists we find in the *American Heritage Dictionary*, in the *NODE* and in the *Wildhagen–Héraucourt* there is only a relatively small overlap.

This is an indication that without suitable corpora, lexicographers are at a loss when it comes to collocations. Even though they are aware of the problem, their findings will be always accidental. Leaving aside, for the moment, the problem of identifying semantically relevant collocations in a monolingual context, we can sketch now what we have to do from a bilingual perspective. We have to look at a corpus. It should be big enough to mirror the kind of language we find in books, newspapers and 'educated speech', i.e. the kind of language we tend to teach in language teaching, and it would yield many more collocations than lexicographers can think of. We would then have to find translations for them. All of those for which the default translation of its elements would be wrong would be entered into the dictionary. We will certainly end up with different sets for each language. In German, a *false alarm* is a *blinder Alarm* (not a *falscher Alarm*); thus this phrase counts as a collocation and belongs in the dictionary. In French, however, it is *alarme fausse*, i.e. the default translation of *alarm* and *false*; and we do not have to treat it as a collocation. If, due to size, not all collocations can be entered into the dictionary, frequency would be an important parameter. We might do without the *false Solomon's seal* and without the *false coral snake*. They seem to be more part of terminology than of the general vocabulary, anyway. *False dawn*, on the other hand, is relatively frequent and would count as a collocation, from a German perspective. The *Oxford–Duden* tells us that its equivalent is: *Zodiakallicht*; (fig.) *Täuschung*. But is *false dawn*, from a monolingual perspective, really a unit of meaning, a single lexical item, or just the combination of two separate lexical items? Can we apply the default meaning test in a monolingual environment?

The *NODE* describes *false dawn* as 'a transient light which precedes the rising of the sun by about an hour, commonly seen in Eastern countries'. According to this definition, *false dawn* seems to be a single lexical item. For we cannot deduce from the meaning of *false* (or from any of the senses a monolingual dictionary may give) and from the meaning of *dawn* (or any of its dictionary senses) that it precedes sunrise by about an hour and that it is specific to Eastern countries (whichever might be meant). But are these really essential or just ornamental features? If they are essential, then *false dawn* is a unit of meaning. For users of the *American Heritage Dictionary*, *false dawn* is described as 'resembling but not accurately or properly designated as the time each morning at which daylight first begins'. This is something that I would be able to deduce from my knowledge of *false* and *dawn*. Here, we are not told that it precedes the real dawn and that it is more commonly found in Eastern countries than elsewhere. If *false dawn* is nothing else, then it is not a unit of meaning. For in this definition, a false dawn resembles a dawn. It is an 'incorrect' dawn. To resolve the issue of the two definitions, let us have a look at the BNC. In the BNC, we find 18 occurrences of *false dawn*. Just two of them refer to a meteorological situation:

> ... it was not until another hour had passed and the moon was paling in the night of the false dawn that they were at last among strange scattered rocks ...

> It was a false dawn, replaced soon after by a now starless night that was blacker than the previous hours.

Neither of these citations mentions an Eastern country, and neither refers to a sunrise occurring an hour later. If these instances are representative, then the *American Heritage Dictionary* seems more reliable, and *false dawn* is not a lexical item. But what about the other occurrences? All of them refer to situations in social life that initially seem to be better than is recognized later. Most commonly these situations refer to economic enterprises. These are some typical citations:

> It is our belief that Christmas will prove to be yet another false dawn as far as reawakening consumer confidence is concerned.

> The organization's chief executive was optimistic that the latest figures did not merely represent another false dawn.

> Unhappily, it was a false dawn.

Google lists ca 1,260,000 hits for the expression *false dawn*. Among the first hits, some citations refer to an economic entity called False Dawn, a book called *False Dawn*, and many instances refer again to situations that appear to be better than later recognized, e.g. the headline: 'Another false dawn for Africa?'. Of course, this meaning of *false dawn* can easily be explained as a metaphor of the *American Heritage Dictionary's false dawn*. Important as this issue of metaphorization is for lexicography, this is not the place to pursue it. But Google gives us as one of the first citations, under www.space.com/spacewatch/zodiacal_light/ the following definition, which ties in nicely with the German equivalent *Zodiakallicht*:

> At certain times of year in the right locations, a faint cone of light appears in the predawn sky for lucky viewers in dark locations. This eerie glow is the Zodiacal Light.
>
> It is best seen before daybreak, generally two to three hours before sunrise in the eastern sky. But it's also visible in the west at certain times of year. Over the centuries countless individuals have been fooled into thinking the Zodiacal Light was the first vestige of morning twilight. In fact, the Persian astronomer, mathematician and poet Omar Khayyam, who lived around the turn of the 12th Century, made reference to it as a 'false dawn' in his one long poem, The Rubaiyat.

If this is what *false dawn* means, then it is a unit of meaning that cannot be reduced to a combination of any of the dictionary senses of *false* and *dawn*. It is a unit of meaning in its own right, a collocation not just on the basis of the frequency of co-occurrence of its elements, but also on the basis of semantic relevance.

When it comes to word-meaning, we are in dire straits. Native speakers understand the meanings of (the more frequent) words of their language. But they are less competent in describing these meanings. This incompetence seems to be shared, to some extent, by the lexicographers. Whatever the reason may be, this may explain why linguistics as we know it has been pre-occupied with grammar. Rules are more elegant than the intricacies of meaning. Rules have explanatory power, they create clarity and understanding, and they provide us with instructions on what to do. There is, however, no rule which could tell us how many senses a word has. The decisions taken are arbitrary. At first glance, it is hard to decide whether it is simply that linguistics has never developed a satisfactory method for dealing with the meanings of words, or whether the situation we are confronted with defies any methodology. Worst of all, the division into different senses seems not to reflect properly how people understand these words when they read them in a text. Experiments have shown that neither lay native speakers nor speakers for whom English is a second language nor trained linguists can easily agree which dictionary sense they should assign to the word in question (Fellbaum 1998; cf. also Edmonds 2002).

How does it come about that highly reputable dictionaries leave such a lot to be desired? There might be a better explanation than incompetence. When we encounter an ambiguous word in a sentence, we normally do not ask ourselves which sense it is used in. Perhaps our understanding of fuzzy words such as *friendly* does not imply putting a given usage into a given pigeonhole. Perhaps our understanding of words is mostly based not on our capacity to categorize, but on our faculty to draw on analogies and to discover resemblances.

Standard linguistics and Chomskyan (or post-Chomskyan) linguistics have not been strong in lexicography. With the demise of philology, the study of the meanings of words has more or less ceased to be a serious academic topic. There is still academic lexicology, and there is semantics; but lexicology has never questioned the categorical approach to word meaning. Rather than describing the meaning of a lexical item as a whole, it has sought to decompose it into more basic semantic features or categories. Many lexicologists still insist that once we get our categories right, better dictionaries will emerge. Semantics, these days, is predominantly cognitive semantics. Cognitive semantics wants to extend Chomsky's claim of the sameness of all languages to meaning as well. These semanticists say that, in principle, we all share the same language, the so-called language of thought, these days often called 'mentalese' (Fodor 1975, Pinker 1994). When we speak, they say, we translate an expression in mentalese into a natural language, and as hearers, we re-translate the natural language expression we hear back into mentalese. This is how Steven Pinker describes this universal mental language:

> People do not think in English or Chinese or Apache; they think in a language of thought. This language of thought probably looks a bit like all these languages; presumably it has symbols for concepts, and arrangements of symbols ... [C]ompared with any given language, mentalese must be richer in some ways and simpler in others. It must be richer, for example, in that several concepts must correspond to a given English word like stool or stud. ... On the other hand, mentalese must be simpler than spoken languages; conversation-specific words and constructions (like a and the) are absent, and information about pronouncing words, or even ordering them, is unnecessary.
>
> (Pinker 1994, pp. 81–2)

Pinker does not tell us, however, how many different concepts correspond to *friendly*, and so we are not told what the universal solution to the categorization of word meanings would look like. It seems that the universality of mentalese is achieved by getting rid of everything which is language specific. There are many languages that do not feature articles, so mentalese does not have them; and languages come up with different word orders, so mentalese does not have information about word order. Pinker is by no means alone in putting his faith in mental representations. He is supported by, among others, Dan Sperber and Deirdre Wilson who discuss the following options: '[T]here are fewer concepts than words', 'there is roughly a one-to-one mapping between words and concepts', and '[m]ost mental concepts do not map into words' (Sperber and Wilson 1998, pp. 186–7). Concepts are more angelic than the earthly words of our natural languages; they seem to avoid the unpleasantness of dealing with the many unpredictable idiosyncrasies of words we find in all the human languages. For cognitive linguists, a word has as many senses as there are concepts into which it translates. Unfortunately there is no dictionary of concepts that lexicographers can consult. Rather, it is the other way around. The so-called conceptual ontologies, which are still popular in artificial intelligence, should be, as their proponents claim, in theory language-independent. How would that be possible? How could we describe the content of a concept without using language? As it is, conceptual ontologies borrow heavily from dictionaries, and there is little hope that it could ever be the other way around. Semantics and lexicology, as they are practised today in the academic world, contribute very little towards an improvement of our dictionaries.

Standard linguistics has brought about better grammars. While it has also brought about a noticeable improvement of dictionaries, particularly of bilingual dictionaries, modern lexicography still falls short of answering our enquiry into the meanings of words in a satisfactory way. The vast majority of people, however, who listen to other people or read their texts, or who try to tell something to other people, do this because they want to understand or be understood. They do not analyse a sentence for the beauty of its syntactic construction, or because they are hunting for a rare species of a verb form. They may not even know that the sentence they have just uttered was in the passive voice. All they want to be sure about is that they, or their listeners, got the meaning right. And here the linguists seem to be unable to help them. They can tell you that 'Paul loves Mary' is (roughly) equivalent to 'Mary is loved by Paul'. But when asked what love means, linguists will refer Mary and Paul to their poor cousins, the lexicographers, who write in the dictionary (in this case the *COBUILD English Dictionary for Advanced Learners*): 'If you love someone, you feel romantically or sexually attracted to someone' or: 'You say that you love someone when their happiness is very important to you, so that you behave in a kind and caring way to them.' If Mary is being told by Paul that he loves her, she finds it important to know what he means by love. She does not have to be aware that the dictionary could inform her about the many senses of this word, which for her is just fuzzy. For her the question is: does Paul only want to go to bed with her, or is he also willing to do the dishes? If Mary grew up in a Western country where English is the native language, she perhaps would not have a problem understanding Paul. But if she came from an Islamic or Hinduistic culture, she might not be acquainted with our kind of love talk. Standard linguistics will not be able to help her. Something new is needed. When we want to find out how language is being used, what words, sentences, texts mean, we have to analyse texts. Looking at the scripts of soap operas, Hollywood movies, novels and magazines read by young people, we can find out what normally happens after a lad says 'I love you'. It is from these soaps, movies, stories, alongside the examples set by his peers, that Paul has learned when to use the phrase himself.

1.4 Corpus linguistics: a different look at language

What is language? Is it the miraculous language faculty we all are born with, which, once it is awakened by verbal contact with native speakers, empowers us to become native speakers as well, and which requires but minimal input to tune the innate mechanism to the specifics of that language? Is it our competence to come up with grammatical sentences that have never been said or heard before? Is there an innate language organ, just as there is an innate capability to see and distinguish colours? If this is what language is, then we have to study it as a feature of the human mind and we do not have to be aware of the rules. They are wired into our brain, and we follow them unconsciously. We also do not have to learn what words mean. Once we are exposed to a word, we relate it to the mental concept into which it translates.

Or is language an acquired skill enabling us to take an active part in verbal communication? Can we learn a language in the same way as we learn to tie our shoelaces, to play chess or to solve equations? This is how we learn to speak a foreign language. We are taught the grammatical and inflectional rules, we are taught the equivalents of the words of our own language in that new language, and vice versa, and in the end we can produce utterances in the new language that comply with what we have learned. It does not really matter if the language we learn really exists, in the sense that there are native speakers. Learning French is hardly different from learning Esperanto, and, in principle, it should not be too different from learning a programming language. If this is what language is, then we take it to be the accumulation of all the instructions needed to speak it competently. If this is what language is, language is not a feature of the mind. Once we have accumulated all the instructions, then there is nothing new to learn about the language.

Or is language something tangible, namely the accumulation of all the acts of communication that took place in a language community, in the same way that British architecture can be seen as the sum of all the buildings that were built in Britain and that we know about? Is the language of the Etruscans or of the Mayans what remains of their texts, or is it the sum of all the acts of communication that ever took place in Etruscan or Mayan? If we accept the latter position, then we can never hope to understand Etruscan or Maya fully. If English is the totality of all acts of communication of the English-language community, of all the texts that exist or have existed at a given time, then language is not a feature of the mind. It is something that exists, in some physical way, something that remains of the recent and the more remote past, something that keeps on growing and developing. If this is the English language, then most of it is lost – most spoken texts, except the very few that were recorded, and many written texts, except those that survive in libraries or in some kind of accessible archive. If we have to restrict our study of English to what is still accessible because it was recorded and preserved, then our picture of English will certainly be much larger than we can ever hope to come to terms with; but it will never be the full picture.

Language is a human faculty which children acquire naturally without being given instructions; it is a set of rules we have learned, from forming plural nouns, to using words in the appropriate order, to following the conventions of letters or essays or reports, and it is a long list of words we have learned (from the simplest of everyday vocabulary to learning that 'an apophthegm is a concise maxim, like an aphorism'). It is also the sum of all texts in that language. In *Macbeth*, IV, iii, 220, Shakespeare uses the verb *dispute* in the sense of 'revenge'. Nobody uses the word like that any more. But this usage has not exactly disappeared. Shakespeare's texts are still a part of our discourse. We read them, we watch his plays, we discuss his language. Thus there are different ways to look at language. It is up to us to decide how we want to study it. It depends on which aspect of language we are interested in. If we want to find out what is common to all languages, we should embrace Chomskyan linguistics. If we want to find out if a French sentence is structured grammatically, we should rely on standard linguistics. If we want to find out what words, sentences and texts mean, we should opt for corpus linguistics.

Corpus linguistics sees language as a social phenomenon. Meaning is, like language, a social phenomenon. It is something that can be discussed by the members of a discourse community. There is no secret formula, neither in natural language nor in a formal calculus, that contains the meaning of a word or phrase. There is no right or wrong. What I call *a weapon of mass destruction* differs probably a lot from what President George W. Bush calls *a weapon of mass destruction*. What I call a *baguette* is not the same as what many supermarkets sell as a *baguette*. What I call *love* may not be what my partner calls *love*. Different people paraphrase words or phrases in different ways. They do not have to agree. In a democracy, everyone's opinion is as good as anyone else's.

Meaning is what can be communicated verbally. If you do not know what *apophthegm* means, you can ask your fellow members of the English discourse community. Many may not be quite sure themselves, and they may refer you to the dictionaries. Someone may quote Samuel Johnson's famous apophthegm 'Patriotism is the last refuge of a scoundrel', and perhaps from then on you will not forget what the word means. The meaning of *apophthegm* for you, then, is the sum of all you have heard from the people you have asked plus all of what you have found in the dictionaries. There is certainly more to the meaning of *apophthegm*. There are more dictionaries that you could consult, there are more people you could ask, there are more texts you could find in libraries and archives containing the word embedded in various contexts. The full meaning of the word is only available once all occurrences of the word in the texts of the English discourse community have been taken into account. All citations together (plus what people tell you when you ask them) are everything one can know about the meaning of *apophthegm*. There is nothing else that could tell us what this word means. And all of it is verbal communication.

The perspective of Chomskyan and cognitive linguistics represents a very different view of language. In that perspective, language is a psychological, a mental phenomenon. Both views are, of course, legitimate, and they are complementary. Corpus linguistics deals with meaning. Cognitive linguistics is concerned with understanding. Meaning and understanding can easily be confused, but it pays to keep them apart. Understanding is something personal, an act that we carry out, both as speakers and as hearers. For cognitive linguists, understanding means translating a word, a sentence, a text into the language of thought, into mentalese. But there remain many unsolved questions. Are all mental concepts universal, including 'bureaucracy' and 'carburettor', which seem to be rather culture-specific? Chomsky thinks there are good arguments to believe that all concepts, including those we are not yet aware of (like future neologisms) are innate (Chomsky 2000, p. 65). Others, like Anna Wierz-bicka, think that only a limited number of basic or primitive concepts are universal and that culture-specific concepts are compositional, in the sense that they are composed of basic concepts. These complex concepts are not universal (Wierzbicka 1996). Jerry Fodor, however, rejects the idea of compositionality (Fodor 1998; Fodor and Lepore 2002).

The unresolved question of the nature of mental concepts is only one of the problems cognitive linguists are confronted with. The other main problem is that of the Aristotelian qualia. Daniel Dennett defines qualia as 'the way things seem to us'. Qualia are 'ineffable' (i.e. they cannot be described), they are 'intrinsic' (internal to the mind) and 'private' (known only to oneself) (Dennett 1993, pp. 65, 338ff.). The image the word *primrose* evokes in my mind is different from the image the same word evokes in your mind. The affective qualities that go with it, i.e. what you feel when you hear the word *primrose*, is something you cannot fully convey to other people. It is difficult to see how the assumption of a universal conceptual basis can be reconciled with the view that understanding is a first-person experience that defies communication. But even if there were a consensus among cognitive linguists about how understanding works, it would still be necessary to set it apart from meaning. Meaning is what we trade in when we communicate; by exchanging content we share it. Thus, cognitive linguistics and corpus linguistics have a different focus of interest. The cognitive sciences are concerned with what happens in the mind in the process of encoding and decoding a message. Corpus linguistics is concerned with the message itself.

Corpus linguistics can tell us more about meaning than either Chomskyan linguistics or standard linguistics. Even so, corpus linguistics can never give us the full

39

picture. If meaning is not a formula, an unambiguous expression in some symbolic calculus (which was what many of the adherents of analytic philosophy were hoping for), if meaning is neither a mental image informed by ineffable qualia, nor a universal concept in a language of thought we know nothing about, if meaning is what can (and must be) conveyed verbally, then meaning is something we can talk about only in natural language. In all probability, we know what the word *school* means not because at some point in our past we looked it up in the dictionary. We know what it means because someone, or, more probably, a number of people, must have told us, in the course of our childhood, what it meant. The people who told us must have learned it the same way. This process, or rather activity, of conveying the meaning has been repeated generation after generation ever since there were schools. If we assemble everything that has been said, in this discourse, about schools, then we have the meaning of *schools*. Not everyone will paraphrase the word *school* for us in the same words. It could well emerge that the common denominator is very small. A good collection of quotations will show this diversity. The following citations are a selection taken from the Bank of English, a 450-million word corpus of English language:

```
       and offers an after- school club. There are infant and
     them in detention after school. Yet pupils in adjoining
       having a tough time at school and came home in tears again
          as they can, because school fees are so unpredictable.
   he was sent to boarding school in England, where he was a
           small private day school in California. There were
     children's camps during school holidays, which include
          at eleven to a grammar school. The rest stayed on at
             And, I'm still in high school!'' While rewarding the first
           university medical school but it could be rented or
      Oxford, said that more school sport is the answer to the
  career after leaving music school to start the family, saw it
       we are a caring sort of school that looks after everybody's
```

```
          written by Head of School, Heather Dixon. 'The two-day
       like some kind of prep school, with its Standing Committee
  currently still at primary school, later gained a place at
     I'll have to go to public school. Iz and Jude say the teachers
    The boy, now 15, skipped school for a year as he took orders
    is practical: 'In Sunday School they told us what you do.
  last night demanded that the school council and head nun Mother
    teenagers. The four go to school, do homework and finish
       said: 'I used to walk to school with Lisa and her children.
```

Corpus linguistics studies languages on the basis of discourse. English discourse is the totality of texts produced, over centuries, by the members of the English discourse community. Even if we confine ourselves to the texts that have been preserved, this discourse is much too large to make it, *in toto*, the object of our research. It will never be possible to study all extant texts. All corpus linguistics can do is to work with a (suitable) sample of the discourse. Such a sample is called the corpus. Because we can never access the whole discourse and not even all extant texts, we can never be sure that what we have assembled as the meaning of a word like *school* will be the full picture. Even more important is the fact that the picture we can deduce from the corpus is full of contradictions. Some like school; others hate it. Some find it useful; for others it is a waste of time. For all lexical items that are worth thinking and talking about, there is hardly a common denominator, there is little agreement. The discourse is not nearly as streamlined as dictionaries want to make us believe. Some lexicographers seem to think that because what we find in our corpus is nothing but an arbitrary and accidental collection of occurrences, this evidence has to be checked by what *school* is in reality, that it is dangerous to rely only on discourse evidence. But if there is a reality outside of the discourse, it has to be turned into a text, it has to become a part of the discourse, so that it can be communicated.

41

We should not, therefore, believe that, if we import information which is not found in our corpus, we are importing discourse-external, factual knowledge. We must not mistake for reality what is outside of our corpus. It is still the discourse. We find, for example, in many dictionaries the custom of adding the Latin name of plant species. Thus the *NODE* tells us the species name of the elm tree is *ulmus*. This has nothing to do with reality. It is information copied from other texts, from Linnaeus's classification of plants and animals. This taxonomy is actually a part of discourse and can be discussed in discourse. But isn't this classification, as many people believe, including philosophers of language, a mirror of reality? Isn't a species the same as the natural kind these philosophers (and many cognitive linguists with them) take for granted? Isn't it a fact that there is a species called *elm* or *ulmus* which would still exist even if there were no humans to give it a name? Isn't it true that a tree either is an elm or it is not, regardless of what you or I happen to believe? Is the category species a concoction of the members of the discourse community, or are there, out there in whatever reality may be, entities that can be classified as belonging to this species or that?

Ernst Mayr, a leading biologist and evolutionist, is deeply sceptical about the reality of natural kinds. He recalls, in his recent book *What Evolution Is*, the history of the species concept:

> Traditionally, any class of objects in nature, living or inanimate, was called a species if it was considered to be sufficiently different from any other similar class ... Philosophers referred to such species as 'natural kinds' ... This typological concept is in conflict with the populational nature of species and with their evolutionary potential.
>
> (Mayr 2002, pp. 165–8)

It seems that the concept of species is, after all, being discussed in uncountable contributions to the discourse. A query in Google for 'definition + species' yields ca 7,230,000 hits. The concept of species or category allows us to put items into a pigeonhole because they share features we think are important. It is a useful device. But we must not forget that we decide which features are so important that the items sharing them belong in the same pigeonhole. George Lakoff, a cognitive linguist widely known for his work on metaphors, gave one of his books the title *Women, Fire, and Dangerous Things*, because one of the four noun classes in the Australian language Dyirbal includes females, fire and dangerous animals (among other things; see Lakoff 1987, pp. 92–104).

The discussion about whether there are elms because we have agreed on calling something an *elm*, or whether we call something *elms* because elms exist in reality goes back to a disagreement between Plato and Aristotle. Platonic realism tells us that there are natural kinds, and we cannot do better but acknowledge them and give them names. According to this view, we would not be able, in the long run, to cope with reality, unless we find out and accept what nature really is. This nature exists independently of our giving names to the entities that it comprises. Aristotelian nominalism disagrees. It holds that people are free to put some things into one pigeonhole and other things into another pigeonhole. It is humans who invent categories to make sense of reality; it is not that they discover categories when they investigate reality. We find it important to distinguish oranges from lemons. Yet for some of us, mandarins, satsumas, tangelos and tangerines are all the same. Do they belong to different categories? Is a morello just a kind of cherry or is it a different fruit?

Wherever in the world analytic philosophy prevails, it seems to go hand in hand with some version or other of realism. Actually, this is not surprising. For analytic philosophers, the important question is this: What has to be the case to make a sentence such as 'This is an elm' or 'This is a morello' true? What makes such a sentence coincide with reality? But to ask this presupposes that there are things out there that are elms. We would have to redefine our concept of truth if elms could be anything that we agree on calling *elms*. Cognitive linguistics holds that if not words then certainly concepts are locked onto things out there in what is called reality (Fodor 1994). Thus cognitive linguistics shows itself to be an offspring of analytic philosophy.

For realists it is therefore very important that the things words stand for really exist and are not just chimeras like the Nazi concept of race. John Searle, a highly distinguished scholar within the philosophy of mind community, tells us in his recent book *Mind, Language and Society*: 'Among the mind-independent phenomena in the world are such things as hydrogen atoms, tectonic plates, viruses, trees and galaxies. The reality of such phenomena is independent of us' (Searle 1998, pp. 13–14). Can we be sure of this? Two hundred years ago, people had never heard about hydrogen atoms, tectonic plates or viruses. But they thought they knew, as a fact, that there was phlogiston, a combustible matter that escapes into the air whenever something is burning. Will we, in another two hundred years, still be happy to describe certain macromolecular structures with an ability to replicate as viruses? Or, for that matter, can we be so sure about the reality of trees? Are there irrefutable criteria to distinguish trees from shrubs or bushes? The *NODE* calls the hazel 'a temperate shrub or a small tree', for the *COBUILD* it is only 'a small tree'. For Germans, it is either a bush (*Haselnussbusch*) or a shrub (*Haselstrauch*), but never a tree. What we call a tree depends, it seems, more on decisions taken by the language community than on facts.

In the Middle Ages a meeting of bishops declared rabbits to be fish. This gave them permission to have rabbit on their Friday menu. Today we are wiser. We know that rabbits belong to the category of rodents. But is this category more real than a category grouping together things that a good Catholic could eat on a Friday? That rabbits belong to the category of rodents seems to be scientifically true, whereas the category of things permitted as food for Fridays is entirely arbitrary and no longer widely accepted. But the Linnean system of classifying plants and animals in terms of relationship and ancestry is not perennial; it became accepted in the Western world in the course of the nineteenth century, and perhaps it will be superseded one day by a new classification based on DNA. Which categorial systems refer more directly to reality, if it is possible to ask such a question?

So if we do not find in our corpus something that tells us what a word means, where are the facts that determine that word's meaning? Facts, as we have seen, only become facts once they are introduced into the discourse. They may be, for all we know, external to the discourse. But it is up to the members of the discourse community to introduce into the discourse what they deem to be facts. The vast majority of things we think are facts, or what we think we know to be true, are things that we have never encountered or investigated personally but have been told about in discourse. For any one of us it is quite impossible to establish a fact without having it negotiated by the discourse. It is the discourse that decides whether a phenomenon is real or not. There may be plenty of facts outside the discourse, but the only facts we can talk about are the ones that have been introduced into the discourse.

It therefore seems obvious that the only source we can ever hope to access about the meaning of a word is the discourse. We cannot hope to make the discourse as a whole accessible to our lexicographic enquiries, but we can compile larger and larger corpora, and we can also use the ever-growing Internet as a virtual corpus. Nevertheless, as new words and phrases are coined day by day, it is conceptually impossible to come up with a corpus that comprises the whole vocabulary of a discourse community. There will always be words which are not contained in our corpus. And there is always the chance to add to our corpus the texts in which these words occur. When it comes to the meaning of words, corpus linguists have to consult their corpus, amend it, consult it again, and so forth, in a Sisyphean effort. What corpus linguists make out as the meaning of words can, thus, never be more than an approximation. A different, a larger corpus can always come up with new paraphrases that were missing from the original corpus.

All communication acts together constitute the discourse of a given discourse community. There is, you could say, a discourse community of all people speaking English. It has existed for centuries, ever since English was around. In it we have the texts written by Geoffrey Chaucer, William Shakespeare, Elizabeth Gaskell and Sylvia Plath, and all the other texts we find in our libraries and archives. We have lost, of course, all the oral communication acts (with the exception of some recent ones) because they could not be recorded, and we have lost most of the unprinted written material, because it was thrown away. All those texts are part of the discourse. We can never study all of it, not even what is extant.

Noam Chomsky and many of his followers have dismissed the corpus as the source of our linguistic knowledge. Language, they say, is productive. With limited means, a finite vocabulary and a manageable set of rules, our language faculty empowers us to generate an infinite number of utterances. All the time, things are being said that have not been said before. Corpus research, they claim, will only tell us what people have said so far. It will not tell us what people are going to say tomorrow. That is certainly true. Corpus linguistics cannot predict language change any better than meteorologists can predict the weather of tomorrow or of next week. When Ted Levitt used *globalization* in the title of an article 'The globalization of markets' he published in the *Harvard Business Review* in 1983, he could not have known, and linguists were not able to predict, that *globalization* would become a keyword of the 1990s (see 2.3 and 2.5).

Generative linguists, however, are not, as we have seen, very much concerned with semantic change. They are interested in grammar. Of course, grammar also changes over time. If we regard quotatives as part of grammar and not of the lexicon, then it is an example of grammatical change that it is now possible to say: 'He comes into the room and he is like "It's much too hot for me in here"', and he turns on the air'. Our old grammars do not list the construction *be like* + direct speech. But is this what the generative grammarians have in mind? What they mean by the generative force of grammar is that using the very same grammar (the grammar of the ideal native speaker), we can produce an infinite set of sentences. This is certainly a true claim, even though Chomsky also admits that 'expressions of natural languages are often unparseable (not only because of length, or complexity in some sense independent of the nature of the language faculty)' (Chomsky 2000). Whatever conforms to rules (some expressions apparently do not) will not be better confirmed by looking at data. More empirical evidence will not make us wiser. Once we have found out that sound travels in standard air at a speed of 330 metres per second, there is no point in examining ever more sound events. If you have learned to inflect Lithuanian nouns with their seven cases correctly, there is absolutely no need to study the inflections of Lithuanian nouns in a corpus. If you know for sure that split infinitives are 'illegal', no amount of split infinitives in your corpus will make them legal. Corpus linguistics should keep its hands off grammar, to the extent that the rules we find in our grammar books are indisputable. (They are not always, though.)

Therefore, in this sense, corpus linguistics is no help when it comes to studying the grammar of a language of which the rules have already been 'discovered'. (However, are these 'discovered' rules always adequate?) But it can tell us more about the meaning of words than standard or Chomskyan linguistics. It extracts from the discourse all that we can find out about meaning. Natural human language is unique in this respect. It is the discourse community that negotiates how words should be used and what they mean. The result of these negotiations is not always agreement. Some people may say that *weapons of mass destruction* is a neutral and unbiased expression; others may say it is derogatory because you only use it for the weapons of your enemy. There seems to be no common understanding what these weapons of mass destruction exactly are, and, consequently, what the phrase *weapons of mass destruction* means. Do cluster bombs belong in that set? What about depleted uranium? We only have to look at the recent discourse to find numerous citations in which people are keen to tell us what they think weapons of mass destruction are. A search in the Bank of English on *weapons of mass destruction* shows us that they stand against the conventional weapons and most commonly mean biological, chemical and nuclear weapons, as in the following citations:

> Terrorists were seeking weapons of mass destruction: chemical, biological and nuclear.

> ...Bush's policy goal of regional security and stability meant eradicating Iraq's capability to build weapons of mass destruction – chemical, biological, and nuclear – ...

> The Security Council is still not satisfied that all weapons of mass destruction, notably biological and chemical arms, have been purged from Iraq...

> The evidence that it is assembling biological, chemical and other weapons of mass destruction is overwhelming.

But the corpus tells us much more than that, it shows us how black and white our world picture is. It tells us that indeed when we talk or write about the weapons of mass destruction, we often mean enemy weapons.

The discourse is full of paraphrases of words and of comments concerning their meaning and the connotations that come with them. Aren't these explanations the kind of information we would like to find when we look up a word or a phrase in the dictionary? Once we take the view that the meaning of words is what members of the discourse community proffer as their meaning, the distinction lexicographers have become attached to, namely the distinction between lexical knowledge and encyclopaedic knowledge, dissolves. Encyclopaedic knowledge is part of our discourse just as much as whatever dictionaries offer as word meanings. The meaning of the phrase *weapons of mass destruction* is what people tell us *weapons of mass destruction* are. Similarly, the true meaning of *water* is not, as the famous American philosopher Hilary Putnam wants us to believe, what water is 'in reality', but what people tell us water is (Putnam 1975, pp. 215–71).

Corpus linguistics questions the position of the

word as the core unit of language. The word is not inherent to language. The Greek word *logos* which we usually believe to be the equivalent of *word* means primarily 'speech' or the 'act of speaking', then 'oral communication', and also an 'expression'. Where it does mean 'word', it means first of all the 'spoken word' (as opposed to *rhema* or *onoma*). Latin *verbum* also means first of all 'expression', 'speech' and 'spoken word'. When we think today of *word*, it seems to be much less a transitory sound event than the written word, something that can easily be identified because it is preceded and followed by a space, a space we normally do not speak or hear. Spaces between written words are a relatively recent invention. It was the monks in the medieval *scriptoria* who introduced them because it made it easier to copy texts. Words are what constitute dictionary entries, and because *weapons of mass destruction* is not a single word, it is hidden away in the dictionary, if it occurs at all. In the *NODE*, the phrase is found under the entry for destruction: 'the action or process of killing or being killed: weapons of mass destruction'.

1.5 A brief history of corpus linguistics

Corpus linguistics is a fairly new approach to language. It emerged in the 1960s, at the same time as Noam Chomsky made his impact on modern language studies. His *Syntactic Structures* appeared in 1957, and while it quickly became a widely discussed text, it was only the publication in 1965 of his *Aspects of the Theory of Syntax* and the subsequent reception of this work that provoked the revision of the standard paradigm in theoretical linguistics. Yet while language theory became increasingly interested in language as a universal phenomenon, other linguists had become more and more dissatisfied with the descriptions they found for the various languages they dealt with. Some of the grammar rules in these descriptions were so obviously violated in all (written) texts that they could not be adequate. Certain features of the language were insufficiently described. For example, there had always been a distinction between transitive verbs and intransitive verbs. This is not enough, however, to describe the number and quality of objects or complements that can depend on a verb. These objects include the direct object, various kinds of indirect objects, prepositional objects and clausal objects, among others. They have to be properly kept apart if we want to describe grammatical structure accurately. For instance, if a verb is turned from active into passive voice, some objects can disappear while others will become subjects. In the 1950s, details such as these raised empirical questions which could not be answered by introspection alone. Real language data were needed.

In the English-speaking world, the first large-scale project to collect language data for empirical grammatical research was Randolph Quirk's Survey of English Usage which later led to what became the standard English grammar for many decades: *A Comprehensive Grammar of the English Language* (Quirk *et al.* 1985). The project kicked off in the late 1950s. It formed a reference point for anyone interested in empirical language studies, including the Brown Corpus to be mentioned below. But at the time, the Survey did not consider computerizing the data. This happened much later, in the mid-1980s, in Quirk and Greenbaum's subsequent project now known as the International Corpus of English (ICE) (http://www.ucl.ac.uk/english-usage/ice/).

Quirk's Survey was a mixture of spoken and written data; there were about 500,000 words of spoken English within a total of one million words. The spoken component was actually the first to be put on a computer, by Jan Svartvik, and became, in the late 1970s, the London Lund

Corpus. It was transcribed in an elaborate way, with much phonological and even phonetic information. It became the first spoken corpus widely available for use, published as a book, though unfortunately still not available as a soundtrack (Svartvik 1990).

The Survey was mostly interested in grammar, not in meaning. Nevertheless, it was one of the very few projects working on empirical data. Due to the pervasiveness of the Chomskyan paradigm, it became increasingly difficult in the 1960s to find acceptance of this kind of data-oriented language research. The Survey was the exception in Britain at that time. Later, in the 1970s, this strand of research was to be taken up by a number of Scandinavian linguists, most of them based in Bergen, Lund and Oslo.

The second data-oriented project in the 1960s was the Brown Corpus, named after Brown University in Providence, Rhode Island, where it was compiled by Nelson Francis and Henry Kučera. The corpus consists of one million words, taken in samples of 2,000 words from 500 American texts belonging to 15 text categories as defined by the Library of Congress. The Brown Corpus was a carefully organized corpus, very easy to use, and proofread until it was almost free of mistakes. So is the similarly composed corpus of British English, the LOB (Lancaster–Oslo–Bergen)–Corpus from the 1970s (Johansson *et al.* 1978). Later, both corpora were manually tagged with part-of-speech information. While it was at first hoped that these corpora would answer questions concerning both the grammar and the lexicon, it was soon realized that a corpus of one million words cannot contain more than a tiny fraction of the whole vocabulary. After the Brown Corpus was compiled and the proofreading was completed, it seemed that linguists, at least in America, lost interest in it. It hardly played a role in transatlantic linguistics, even though it became a popular resource in European linguistics. The LOB–Corpus was exploited in subsequent corpus studies, for research into grammar and, more importantly, into word frequency, but not into meaning, mostly in co-operation between British and Scandinavian scholars, including Geoffrey Leech, Knut Hofland and Stig Johansson.

It seems it was Nelson Francis who was the first to apply the term *corpus* to his electronic collection of texts. John Sinclair believes this is how the new usage may have originated:

> There is a story that Jan Svartvik tells about him [Nelson Francis] coming to London with a tape containing the Brown Corpus or part of it and meeting Randolph Quirk there in the mid sixties. Nelson threw this rather large and heavy container, as tapes were then, on Quirk's desk and said: 'Habeas corpus'. Francis also uses *corpus* in the title of his collection of texts, i.e. the Brown University Corpus, and as such it is referred to in the OSTI Report.
>
> (Interview with John Sinclair in Krishnamurthy, 2004)

A third, and certainly most important, early corpus project was English Lexical Studies, begun in Edinburgh in 1963 and completed in Birmingham. The principal investigator was John Sinclair. It was he who first used a corpus specifically for lexical investigation, and it was he who took up the novel concept of the collocation, introduced in the 1930s by Harold Palmer and A. S. Hornby in their *Second Interim Report on English Collocations* (1933), and then taken up by J. R. Firth in his paper 'Modes of meaning' (Firth 1957). This project investigated, on the basis of a very small electronic text sample of spoken and written language, amounting to not even one million words, the meaning of 'lexical items', a term that included collocations. John Sinclair's final report,

English Lexical Studies (often referred to as the OSTI-Report), was distributed in no more than a handful of typewritten copies in 1970. It was often referred to in later studies, but has only recently been published properly for the very first time (Krishnamurthy 2004). At the time, Sinclair had not yet completely abandoned the notion of the word as the unit of meaning, but he was keen to modify the traditional view of the word as the core unit. Still, while the project participants explored the relationship between the word and the unit of meaning, there was no clear appreciation of semantic units as multi-word units with their variations stretching across the phrases. A beginning had nevertheless been made.

Unfortunately, in the 1970s, 1980s and even 1990s, the quest for meaning all but disappeared from the agenda of the newly established corpus research. This is not as astonishing as it sounds. After all, compiling corpora, particularly larger ones, posed a host of problems, mostly technical ones, but also the still-popular question of representativeness. Was there a corpus that could be said to represent the discourse? Was it possible to define text types, domains or genres in general terms? Was there a recipe for the composition of what came to be called a reference corpus? How important was size? What was the role of special corpora? (See 2.1 and 2.2.)

Standardization also became an issue of overriding importance for the 1980s and 1990s. How should corpora be encoded? Was it permissible to add corpus-external information in the form of annotation or tagging? Could there be a common tag-set for all languages? Wouldn't using annotated corpora mean that you only extract from them what you first added to them, thus perpetuating possible misconceptions?

Then there is the question of frequency. With corpora, it was, for the first time, possible to come up with lists of the most frequent words accounting for the basic vocabulary. Everything could be counted and compared: verb–complement constructions, the distribution of the various relative pronouns, or the position of adjectival modifiers in late Middle English noun phrases. Register variation of different Englishes is still a common topic of many corpus studies. Frequency information could also shed new light on grammatical rules. It became possible to investigate the relationship between rare events and a decrease of linguistic competence, of what one could say and what one would say. In this sense, frequency data could be used to revise our view of syntax.

If we look at the papers from the 13th and 14th International Conferences on English Language Research on Computerised Corpora (Aarts *et al.* 1992; Fries *et al.* 1993), organized by the venerable ICAME association, these were very much the topics presented there. The papers deal with creating corpora, with corpus design questions, with annotation, with language varieties and with parsing techniques. Among the 38 papers presented at the two conferences, perhaps four or five focus on collocational aspects of language and only one explicitly deals with semantic issues: Willem Meijs on 'Analysing nominal compounds with the help of a computerised lexical knowledge system'. Here, too, then, we learn very little about extracting meaning from the corpus, and more about assigning predefined semantic features from a conceptual ontology to collocations found in the corpus.

It is not astonishing that the final report *Towards a Network of European Reference Corpora* (finally published in 1995) of the 1991/92 European Commission project talks about user needs, corpus design criteria, encoding, annotation and even knowledge extraction, but does not touch on meaning as a possible focus of

55

corpus research (Calzolari *et al.* 1995). Even the intro-
ductions to corpus linguistics which appeared in the
1990s refrain from devoting much space to the corpus-
oriented study of meaning. Tony McEnery and Andrew
Wilson (McEnery and Wilson 1996) may serve as one
example. Forty pages of their book are devoted to
encoding, 20 pages deal with quantitative analysis, 25
pages describe the usefulness of corpus data for computational linguistics and 30 pages cover the use of corpora
in speech, lexicology, grammar, semantics, pragmatics,
discourse analysis, sociolinguistics, stylistics, language
teaching, diachrony, dialectology, language variation
studies, psycholinguistics, cultural anthropology and
social psychology. The final 20 pages present a case
study on sub-languages and closure. In Graeme Kennedy's introduction to corpus linguistics (Kennedy 1998)
30 pages out of 300 are devoted to 'lexical description',
including 12 pages on collocation. Unsurprisingly, for
Kennedy lexical description seems to be more or less
synonymous with frequency information. In their book of
similar size *Corpus Linguistics: Investigating Language
Structure and Use* (also 1998) Douglas Biber, Susan
Conrad and Randi Reppen again have about 30 pages on
'lexicography'. The two basic questions they address are:
'How common are different words? How common are the
different senses for a given word?' (Biber *et al.* 1998, p.
21). This looks like frequency analysis together with the
belief that word senses are somehow discourse external
and can be assigned to lexical items. But at least they
mention, on two pages, the relevance of the context for
determining senses. The rest of the section is devoted to
an investigation into the distribution of the word *deal*,
with its various senses, over the registers of different text
genres. In the absence of an introduction dealing explicitly with matters of meaning, John Sinclair's *Corpus
Collocation Concordance* (1991) filled the gap, until

Michael Stubbs' *Words and Phrases: Corpus Studies of Lexical Semantics* was published in 2001.

There was, however, a large corpus-based dictionary project, the *Collins COBUILD English Language Dictionary*, conceived and designed in the mid-1970s and published in 1987, under the guidance of John Sinclair. The story of this venture is told in *Looking Up: An Account of the COBUILD Project in Lexical Computing*, also published in 1987. This was the first ever general language dictionary based exclusively on a corpus. Therefore, the corpus had to be big enough to include all the lemmas and all the word senses the dictionary assigned to these lemmas. A consequence is that rare words, like *apo(ph)thegm*, are missing. They were not in the corpus. However, except in cases of doubt, the lexicographers did not use corpus information to carve up the meaning of a word into its senses; rather, the corpus was used in the first place to validate the lexicographers' decision and to provide examples. More could not be done with this corpus of 18.3 million words (Birmingham Collection of English Text), then the largest general language corpus in the world. From today's point of view, collocations are not given the prominence they ought to have. Dictionary publishers have not been keen on collocation dictionaries. In many ways, the *COBUILD* dictionary is still unique. While it encouraged other dictionary makers to include more corpus evidence, there is still no other dictionary exclusively based on a corpus.

Elena Tognini-Bonelli distinguishes between the corpus-based and the corpus-driven approaches (Tognini-Bonelli 2001). Linguistic findings (including the contents of dictionaries) are corpus-based if everything that is being said is validated by corpus evidence. Findings are corpus-driven if they are extracted from corpora, using the methodology of corpus linguistics, then intellectually processed and turned into results. This is a crucial distinction. The corpus-based approach will deliver only results within the framework of standard linguistics. It can show that one of the five senses normally listed for *friendly* does not occur at all in the corpus, and that in addition to the five senses, there is another usage that has been overlooked by other dictionaries. It will not show that you can get rid of most of the ambiguity by identifying the collocates of *friendly* and making these collocations your lemmas. If corpus linguistics is really going to complement standard linguistics rather than just extend it, it must follow the corpus-driven, not the corpus-based approach. This is what we aim to demonstrate in the following chapter.

2 Directions in corpus linguistics

Wolfgang Teubert and
Anna Čermáková

2.1 Language and representativeness

Ever since linguists started using corpora they have been thinking hard about how corpora should be composed. The corpus should represent the discourse, or some predefined section of it. What the Brown Corpus represented was the English language of the year 1961, in print, as catalogued by the Library of Congress. In this corpus, each publication is assigned to one of 15 content categories. The catalogue for the publications of 1961 represents this discourse. It tells us how many texts were published within each of the categories, and these figures were used as guidelines to select the texts. From each of the 500 texts chosen, a 2,000-word sample was then entered into the corpus. This selection process can be operationalized, turned into unambiguous, clear instructions, and is therefore objective. But is the corpus representative?

It represents, in a rather loose way, the Library of Congress catalogue. That is not the same, though, as the discourse constituted by all the printed publications of the USA in 1961. The 15 categories into which the catalogue entries are divided are arguable. You could have more or fewer, and the subject fields could be defined quite differently. A few centuries ago, there would have been a category for alchemy and one for astrology, but none for economics. The whims of people change. Depending on the number and content of these basic categories, one might come up with an entirely different selection of texts for our corpus, a selection which was in every respect as objective as that of the Brown Corpus.

Then there is the question of readership. In a catalogue, a newspaper with a circulation of several million copies has an entry comparable to a book printed in 120 copies. But is the number of readers important? What really determines the importance of a text. Who wrote it? How many copies circulated? How many people read it? Is it right to include only printed and published texts and thus to exclude perhaps more than 90 per cent of what makes up the discourse of any given year: informal conversations within the family, in schools, in bars, cafes and clubs, with friends on an outing, at the workplace; the letters we receive, the advertisements we read, the reports, minutes and memos we find on our desks, to name but a few?

There are wider questions. Are English texts published

outside of the USA, but found on the shelves of the Library of Congress, part of the American discourse? What about books published by Americans who live outside the USA? Does American English include, for example, the English spoken by immigrants in the USA or the English of Puerto Ricans? What exactly is the discourse?

A language, a discourse, consists of the totality of verbal interactions that have taken place and are taking place in the community where this language is spoken. This community we call the discourse community. Language communities can be small. Some are so small, in fact, that their languages have become endangered, or even extinct as with many of the Uralic (Finno-Ugrian) languages. There are (or were) languages spoken by only a dozen people or even fewer. Manx, for example, died out a few decades ago; at the end, there was only one (native) speaker left, conversing in Manx only with the handful of linguists specializing in this Celtic language. Other language communities are so large and diverse, like the community of English-language speakers, that it does not seem proper from a sociological perspective to call them communities at all.

The totality of the verbal interactions of a specific language community includes idiolects, sociolects, dialects, regional variants, languages for special purposes, eighteenth-century language and contemporary language, female language and male language, slang and jargon, and innumerable other kinds of language we can sometimes distinguish.

Languages and discourse communities do not exist as such. They are social constructs. We construe them to suit our purposes. Until the dissolution of the old Yugoslavia, most of us believed there was a language called Serbo-Croatian. Now there are books telling us that such a language never existed, and that Serbian and Croatian were always distinct languages. Nowadays words considered to be originally Serbian (or even Turkish) are purged from Croatian and replaced by newly coined words built from 'purely' Croatian morphemes. Half a century ago the Northern Indian lingua franca Hindustani (a pidgin that become a Creole) was replaced by Hindi and Urdu. Both of these were originally at least as artificial as Hindustani, yet today, thanks to massive political intervention, they are irrefutably natural languages in their own right and to a large extent mutually incomprehensible. Germans normally do not understand spoken Swiss German, but tradition has it that it is the same language. Slovaks and Czechs do not need interpreters to understand each other, but historical and political circumstances have enforced the notion that they are two separate languages. There is no formula telling us what a language is and what a language community is. It is up to us to design our formula in agreement with our intentions. We define languages and language communities according to experience, according to what seems useful at a given time.

Discourse communities may be social constructs, but we do experience them as real. The members of a discourse community negotiate who belongs to it and who does not. There are thousands of texts telling us, as a 'fact', how many speakers there are for English, or Chinese or Manx. The discourse itself is unfathomable, inexhaustible and, as a whole, inexplorable. Perhaps we can approach the conundrum of representativeness more easily if we approach it from the other end, from the corpus.

In the words of John Sinclair (1991) a corpus is 'a collection of naturally occurring language text, chosen to characterize a state or variety of a language'. The texts are all samples, cross-sections of the discourse. But sampling the discourse can mean different things. If we look at the discourse of written English texts, we could, if we chose to, say that a representative corpus is one that reflects the frequencies and proportions of all the 26 letters plus the special characters like punctuation marks and the space in between words. Is that what we should call a representative corpus?

Perhaps, though, we are interested not so much in the frequency of letters as in the frequency of words. Let us assume, again, that there are half a million words in English (the number does not matter, really, because we will not agree on the definition of word). Some of these half-million words are very frequent, such as the function words (*a*, *the*, *to*, etc.; see 1.1); some of them are quite frequent (say, the 20,000 or so headwords you would find in a typical pocket dictionary); and the rest of them are rather less frequent. The most frequent word in English is the definite article *the* and nearly all of the most frequent hundred words are function words such as pronouns and prepositions. Among the most frequent words, there are only a very few nouns and verbs which can be said to have a meaning of their own, and all of these words are highly ambiguous or fuzzy (words like *thing* or *set*). All words are part of the discourse; they all have been used at least once. But no matter how large our sample of the discourse is, we will miss most of them. There is no occurrence of my favourite word *apophthegm* in the 450-million-word Bank of English. This is purely accidental. There are, on the other hand, many thousands of other words nobody has ever heard of, words occurring only once in the corpus, for example *abelch*, *airpad*, *eurocrisis* and *keyphone*. Such a word, for which we have no more than one citation, is called a *hapax legomenon* (Greek: 'read only once'). Some of these words may be misspellings but many may be real words.

Therefore, talking about the frequency of words, we just may be able to say that a corpus represents a discourse, inasmuch as the 10,000 most frequent words of the discourse are also the 10,000 most frequent words of the corpus. The presence or absence of words less frequent is as unpredictable as the winning numbers in a lottery. But even if we only consider the most frequent part of the vocabulary we find ourselves at a loss.

In whatever way we look at the question of representativeness, we will always have to define what it is that our corpus is to represent. As long as we have not defined what the discourse is which we want to represent, we just do not know what the 10,000 most frequent words are. Nor do we know how different domains (such as politics, gardening, property law or rugby) are distributed over the discourse. The same is true for genres, based on text-external classification (fiction, newspaper language, academic writing, appliance instructions, poetry), or text types, based on text-internal features (containing first person singular, past tense, passive, quotations, etc.), and for registers (e.g. formal, informal, technical, derogatory, vulgar language).

There have been many attempts to define the discourse, and the catalogue of the Library of Congress is just one example. You might want to compile a corpus representing the discourse of Australian English of the year 2000. Since we cannot hope to have easy access to spoken texts, let us restrict our discourse to written texts. Let us also exclude, for the moment, unpublished written texts. We thus narrow our definition of the discourse for which we want to compile a corpus down to the totality of written English texts, published in Australia in the chosen year. Is that what we want? Let us further assume we have agreed on what to do with texts by Australians published outside Australia and texts by non-Australian English writers published within Australia, and that we have agreed upon the relationship of writing texts (sampling authors) to reading texts (sampling readers). There are still other parameters such as gender, educational background and age of writer and/or of reader. Probably for a country like Australia, some linguists are also interested in the ethnic backgrounds of the writers/readers of texts. These are parameters defining the discourse community, and not the discourse. Are these parameters we should be interested in?

In any case, we are only justified in claiming that a given corpus is representative of a discourse, however we have defined it, if we have, at least in principle, access to all the texts the discourse consists of. Only then will we have all the relevant information concerning the parameters mentioned above, and only then can we be sure that the corpus we compile as a sample of this discourse is representative, at least in respect to the parameters mentioned above. But if this utopia came true, we could well do without the corpus. We would already have the discourse as a whole and would not need to sample it. We would have no need to work with a sample. We could work with the whole discourse. Perhaps in a decade or two it will be possible to access all the written texts published in Australia in a given year. But presumably it will never be possible to enumerate all the spoken and written texts of the Australian discourse of a given year as a whole. This is why it does not make much sense to talk about representativeness.

2.2 Corpus typology

2.2.1 Reference corpus

However, this might not be at all what we mean when we discuss the representativeness of a corpus of British, Australian or American English. Fortunately, these discourse communities have discussed at length what they mean by standard English. There is a good measure of agreement about what kind of English we should teach to foreigners. Of course, these attitudes have changed in the course of history. A century ago, languages were mostly taught on the basis of 'good' literature, including novels and non-fiction books on certain cultural and historical topics. Today we think the register to be taught should also include the kind of spoken language used by the educated middle classes. This is not the most numerous segment of society, but, in the eyes of the discourse community, it is the most prominent or significant. We could also define as standard English the private annual reading load of educated middle-class citizens. This might consist of a larger share of broadsheets and a smaller one of tabloids, amounting to probably 50 per cent of the total, perhaps another 10 per cent consisting of the weekly and monthly periodicals we subscribe to, perhaps 25 per cent consisting of fiction and non-fiction books we read through the year, and the remaining 15 per cent an odd mixture of brochures, instruction leaflets and sundry printed material we come across, from tax forms and telephone bills to tourist brochures and theatre programmes. We could include, in proportion, children's literature. There is no cogent reason to exclude our professional reading load, but many people, including many linguists, would think that these texts are too diverse and too far away from what we usually read that they would not belong to any common ground. The language of a medical journal, of aircraft maintenance manuals or the customs regulations, for example, is not part of my linguistic repertoire. Our corpus thus comes to consist of what the members of the discourse community have agreed to be representative of standard (British, Australian or American) English. For the reasons discussed above, we should not call a corpus which represents such a socially accepted standard a representative corpus. These days, corpus linguists prefer to call such a corpus a reference corpus.

Today, corpus linguists would expect a national language reference corpus to comprise between 50 million and 500 million words, if not more. There are perhaps one or two dozen languages for which reference corpora of this (or larger) size already exist or are under construction. For German, there is the IDS (Institut für Deutsche Sprache) corpus with more than a billion words; there is the Språkbanken Swedish corpus of 75 million words and the Czech National Corpus of 200 million words; and there are two large reference corpora for English, the 100-million word British National Corpus and the 450-million word Bank of English. Reference corpora of different languages are comparable if they are similar in size and if their composition is similar in respect to genres and/or other parameters. The PAROLE corpora of all official EU languages, for example, are comparable in this sense, but, given today's standards, they are rather small – not more than 20 million words per language.

Reference corpora are being used for a multitude of purposes. Reference corpora contain the standard vocabulary of a language. They are the corpus linguist's main resource to learn about meaning. If they are large enough, they reveal the contexts into which words are usually embedded, and with which other words they form collocations. Only in corpora of this size can we detect these units of meaning that are so much more telling than single words, with their ambiguities and fuzziness. We need reference corpora, the larger the better, for investigating lexical semantics. A typical reference corpus will represent what the discourse community agrees to be what a fairly educated member of the middle class would read outside of work, mostly in printed form, but also handwritten or typed; and, in principle at least, it should also contain a sample of what they would hear, in conversation, at more formal social events, or on the radio. It is carefully construed, with a deliberate composition.

67

The British National Corpus of 100 million words, compiled in the early 1990s, is a good example (http://www.natcorp.ox.ac.uk/).

Reference corpora, however, also serve another purpose. They can be used as benchmarks for special corpora. Whenever we do not want to look at standard language as a whole but at some special phenomenon we happen to be interested in, we usually have to compile a corpus that fits our research focus. Such a corpus is called a special corpus. Special corpora are sometimes quite small, under a million words, though they can be much bigger of course. Let us assume, for the moment, we are interested in the collocation *friendly fire*. Our research questions are: How quickly did this neologism spread after it was first coined in 1976? How was it paraphrased? Are people aware of the inherent irony? Are there different usages? Does it occur only in talking about the military, or are there other domains in which we now use *friendly fire*? When did the expression pick up in British English? What was *friendly fire* called before the expression was coined? What happened to that word? If this is the set of questions to which we want to find answers, we have to compile an appropriate corpus. It must include texts from 1976 onwards. In order to find out the frequency over longer periods of time, we must set up subcorpora for different phases, say for 1976–8, 1980, 1985, 1990 and 2000. These subcorpora have to be identical in size and in composition so that it really makes sense to compare frequencies. The easiest way to come up with such a set of comparable subcorpora is to take newspapers. So perhaps we should take *USA Today*, the *Washington Post*, the *Los Angeles Times*, the *Burlington Intelligencer* and the *Springfield Examiner*, for the years we want to look at. Where do we find these newspapers and their text files? Some papers publish all the year's texts in annual CDs, which can be bought. In other cases, we may have to contact the publisher. If we cannot get a paper, we must find a suitable substitute. We should look around for databanks on the Internet containing this kind of material. Do we need the whole newspaper? In fact, we could reduce the size of the corpus by selecting only those articles in which the phrase occurs. Or should we just take the sentences containing *friendly fire*? Better not, for it may well be that relevant semantic information may be found in the wider context. Can we leave out certain sections, such as sport? Not if they contain the phrase. We then have to compile a very similar corpus of British newspapers, to be able to find similarities and differences. If our British corpus includes the (London) *Times* of 2 November 2001, we will find the following citation:

> Blair's war effort is put under friendly fire. Labour rebels, disgruntled backbenchers, forced the first Commons vote on the conflict in Afghanistan.

This citation tells us a number of things: first of all, *friendly fire* is also used in British English. Second, the phrase is also used in the political domain. Third, if used outside of the military domain, we also find a metaphorical usage. These backbenchers do not use guns or missiles; they use their right to vote. And finally, there is a semantic difference that comes with metaphorization: this friendly fire is no longer accidental; it is intentional.

There is no standard recipe for the composition of a special corpus. All we have to do is to draw up a set of hypotheses that will guide us in defining the special corpus we need. It may well turn out that in the course of our inquiry, our hypotheses have to be modified. This may mean it becomes necessary to extend our corpus. It is always possible to add to it. Corpora are by no means sacrosanct. They are the corpus linguists' creation, and they can do with them whatever they deem reasonable.

An alternative to the reference corpus is the opportunistic (or cannibalistic) corpus. The opportunistic corpus does not claim to represent a language or to mirror a discourse; an opportunistic corpus is based on the assumption that each and every corpus is imbalanced. Once we take for granted that corpora are inherently imbalanced, we are free to tackle the problem of representativeness or balance from a different angle. This new perspective is the strict separation of corpus compilation from corpus application. The opportunistic corpus is the result of collecting all the corpora one can lay hands upon. Almost all of these corpora will be special corpora; but there may also be a few that call themselves reference corpora. The larger the opportunistic corpus is, the better it is. But the best opportunistic corpus is also the one that is documented in the most comprehensive way.

Therefore we first have to define the genres, domains and text types, and in doing so we have to take into consideration two aspects. One aspect is what possible users of our opportunistic corpus might want to look for. What are the genres, domains and text types that have been discussed and analysed by linguists? This should be the starting point of our own classification. The other aspect is what kind of information we can hope to find in any corpus we want to add to our opportunistic corpus. Will there be any genre/domain/text type information, either in the texts or attached to them, that we can retrieve automatically and include in the documentation files? This is an important question because the integration of a new corpus into an existing opportunistic corpus should be done as automatically as possible. What we also need is, for each text, the date of its publication, the name and details of the author, its title and all the other information one would like to put into a bibliography. An ideal opportunistic corpus is a corpus in which this kind of information is available for each text of each of the corpora it is composed of.

Once there is a sufficiently large opportunistic corpus available, people who want to use corpora for their research can query the documentation in order to identify the texts they would like to use. Someone working on the vocabulary of Victorian novels would select all the relevant novels they would find in the opportunistic corpus, and leave the rest aside. Another project might be an exploration of the special language of sport. Opportunistic corpora will contain a lot of newspaper material, and again the thorough documentation of all texts will make it very simple to select the ones we are interested in, i.e. the sport sections of the newspapers, plus whatever other material is classified as belonging to the domain of sports. There will always be research topics for which an opportunistic corpus does not provide the basis. The larger it grows, however, the wider will be the variety of research purposes it fits. Indeed, whenever people maintaining an opportunistic corpus come across some special corpus which could be useful for a future research agenda, it should be added. Opportunistic corpora are principally open-ended. The corpus holdings of the Mannheim Institut für Deutsche Sprache, now running at more than two billion words and still growing rapidly, are currently the largest opportunistic corpus.

2.2.2 Monitor corpus

The monitor corpus is a corpus that monitors language change. It is, in principle, regularly updated and open-ended. Corpus linguistics is particularly interested in lexical change, such as:

- the change of frequency of words or other units of meaning (compounds, multi-word units, collocations, set phrases), which is often indicative of a change in meaning or a change in the domains in which words are used;

- the occurrence of new words;
- the occurrence of new larger units of meaning;
- changing context profiles, i.e. changes in the frequencies of words occurring in the contexts of words or other units of meaning.

The introduction of new words into the discourse is the most obvious, but not the most frequent lexical change. Studies undertaken for a German newspaper (the *Süddeutsche Zeitung*, Munich) have shown that the majority of new character strings in between blanks, i.e. strings that have not been previously registered, are first typing errors and then names of persons, organizations and geographical units, then abbreviations. The small remainder (about 15 items per day) consists of previously unrecorded forms of words already registered, ad hoc compounds (which are written in one word in German) and every now and then a true neologism.

Monitor corpora should, as much as possible, adhere to the same initial composition. As far as they consist of newspapers and periodicals, this should not be difficult. Newspapers tend to develop their own unique styles, and this style manifests itself in a specific vocabulary. Comparing this week's *Daily Telegraph* with last week's *Guardian* yields unreliable evidence. What is new for one paper may have been another paper's common usage for a long time. A corpus of nothing but newspapers and periodicals seems to be somewhat unsatisfactory. We would like to include other genres, as well. But what do we achieve, in terms of documenting lexical change, by randomly selecting, say, ten fiction and ten non-fiction books per annum? Novels as well as popular science or history books tend to have a specific topic. A single book on tennis would change the frequency of tennis terminology for this monitor corpus year to such an extent that it would bias the results. Such a slant could be set off only if we added not ten but hundreds of books per year. A compromise would be to include a book review journal like the *Times Literary Supplement*. A book review will normally contain the new vocabulary that comes with the book, but not to such an extent that it will bias frequency counts. Unfortunately, large-scale monitor corpora reflecting what is seen as standard written language are still not available. However, this situation will change over the next few years.

2.2.3 Parallel corpora

A parallel corpus, sometimes also called a translation corpus, is a corpus of original texts in one language and their translations into another (or several other languages). Reciprocal parallel corpora are corpora containing original texts and translated texts in all languages involved. Sometimes parallel corpora contain only translations of the same texts in different languages, but not the text in the original language. Such a corpus can tell us how the English we find in translations differs from authentic English. Sometimes it is not known – or it is thought to be irrelevant – which text is the original and which text is the translation. For example, we are not told in which language legal documents issued by the European Commission are drawn up. It used to be mostly French, but more recently the final version has often been in English, and it can well happen that previously working versions were drafted in other languages. The same is true for texts issued by the Vatican. These days a long time has passed since Latin was the original version. The languages are mostly Italian and French but also English, Spanish and German, and the Latin version is added at a later stage. These parallel corpora cannot tell us how French texts are translated into English, but they can show in which cases the word *travail* (or its plural *travaux*) is equivalent to *work*, and in which cases to *labour* or other expressions.

Parallel corpora are repositories of the practice of translators. The community of translators from language A to language B and vice versa know a lot more about translation equivalence than can be found in any (or all) of the bilingual dictionaries for these languages. Even the largest bilingual dictionary will present only a tiny segment of the translation equivalents we find in a not-too-small parallel corpus. Because the ordering principle of printed dictionaries is alphabetical, based on mostly single-word entries, bilingual dictionaries do not record larger and more complex units of meaning in a methodical way. Neither do they tell us which of the equivalents they offer belong in which contexts. This is one of the reasons why bilingual dictionaries do not help us to translate into a language we are not very familiar with. The user is left with many options and hardly any instructions for selecting the proper equivalent. From parallel corpora we can extract a larger variety of translation equivalents embedded in their contexts, which make them unambiguous. This is what makes parallel corpora so attractive. Working with parallel corpora lets us do away with ambiguity, with being given alternatives between which we have to choose. We will identify monosemous units of meaning in one language and find the equivalents in the other language(s). Now, when we have to translate a given word, we will compare this word with the words we find in its company, with the words in the units of meaning we have extracted from the parallel corpus. The closest match usually renders the correct translation equivalent.

For most applications, parallel corpora will have to be aligned so that a unit in one language corresponds to the equivalent unit in another language. The standard unit of alignment is still the sentence. In the beginning, parallel corpora were sentence-aligned by hand. For alignment is not a trivial task. First, it is not always easy to identify sentence endings automatically. Full stops can also designate abbreviations, some of which can occur either within a sentence or at the end, such as *etc.* In some languages, full stops can also indicate ordinal numbers (2. = 2nd). Second, sentences are by no means stable units. One sentence in the source language can correspond to two or more sentences in the target language; or two source language sentences can be subsumed in one target language sentence. Anyone who has closely compared texts and their translations will have noticed that sometimes sentences are plainly omitted in the translation, or that new sentences are introduced, it seems, almost at the translator's whim. This is why, even though there are various tools available to align corpora on the sentence level, alignment is a time-consuming process involving substantial human intervention. This is one of the reasons why there are still only a few parallel corpora of considerable size (say, more than 5 million words per language).

It is even trickier to align corpora on the lexical level. Ideally, one would like to see each unit of meaning in the source corpus linked to the equivalent unit in the target corpus. (Source and target, in this context, do not refer to the language of the original and the translated text; rather, the source language is the language which we choose as our point of departure, while the target language is the one in which we want to find equivalents.) Our results will, to a certain extent, depend on this directionality. It is well known that bilingual dictionaries are not reversible. Whether the results extracted from a parallel corpus are reversible, and to what extent, is still unknown. Lexical alignment uses statistical procedures and/or lexicon look-up. Neither is very reliable. It is because bilingual dictionaries (and the lexicons derived from them) are not very instructive that we turned to parallel corpora in the first place. Hence the lexical alignment we start with is only tentative; and all it tells us is what could be an equivalent of the source unit. We will still be given both *work* and *labour* and also some other words like *employment* or *job* as equivalent of French *travail*. If we want to find out more, we have to look at the contexts in which *travail* is embedded when it is translated as *work*, as opposed to the contexts in which *travail* is embedded when it is translated as *labour*. Thus, if we have to translate *travaux* followed by the adjective *préparatoires*, our parallel corpus tells us that this phrase is never translated as *preparatory labours* but always as *preparatory work* (with a singular phrase in English corresponding to the French plural phrase).

2.2.4 Internet corpus

Recently it has become quite common among corpus linguists to consult the Internet as a virtual corpus. This is particularly useful when we want to find out if a word or a phrase we have heard really exists and in which kinds of texts it occurs. Whenever we cannot find evidence of words or units of meaning in our classic corpora, we can turn to the Internet. There are many commercial browsers we can use, like Altavista or Google, and they all have their advantages and disadvantages. The Internet is larger than any existing library, and if a word is in current use, we are bound to find it there. What we do not know, however, is how the Internet is composed in terms of the parameters mentioned earlier. Frequencies of occurrence have to be carefully interpreted. The Internet can be seen neither as a sample of a middle-class person's private reading load nor as a sample of text production *in toto.* So far, there are very few transcripts of spoken language on the Internet, and the written language we find is a reflection of what kind of texts different people put on the Internet. Some texts exist only there; others are copied from other written material. And here too we must be careful; not all copies are perfect clones of the original texts.

For practical purposes, the Internet, even if we restrict ourselves to the freely accessible websites, is, at any given time, if not infinite then certainly inexhaustible. No browser can claim to cover all the existing web pages. Such a selection is usually so big that by the time we have extracted all citations for a given keyword (or larger unit of meaning), some texts queried will already have been taken from the servers they were on, while others, new ones, will have been added. The Internet is a virtual corpus, and, like the discourse of any language community, we cannot expect to access it as a whole. Normally, if someone wants to use the Internet as a source, they should, therefore, download all the texts they are working with, and compile them in a special corpus; and they should document them with their web addresses and other bibliographic information and the date of the download.

2.3 Meaning in discourse

'When I use a word,' Humpty Dumpty said in a rather scornful tone, 'it means just what I choose it to mean – neither more nor less.'

'The question is,' said Alice, 'whether you can make words mean so many different things'.

'The question is,' said Humpty Dumpty, 'which is to be the master – that's all.'

(Lewis Carroll, *Alice Through The Looking Glass*)

It is not Humpty Dumpty as an individual but the discourse community as a whole (or at least sufficiently significant fractions of it) that decide what a word means. Individual members of this community who want to say something but are dissatisfied with the words they find and how they are being used, have two options. They can either introduce a new word (e.g. *Eurotrash*, the name of a popular series on British television) into the discourse – which happens relatively rarely – or they can try to change the meaning of an existing word, by using it in a new context. Shifts in the meaning often start off in slang: today's slang use of *wicked* means 'good', while the 'proper' meaning is quite the opposite. The meaning of the word *tart* as 'woman of loose morals' has become so dominant that bakeries and cafes sometimes see themselves pressed to use new (and no doubt more elegant) names like *gateau* and *torte*. Another example is the *cold caller* (most neologisms appear to be collocations of some sort or other), who is not a caller in the cold, but someone who is paid for calling people they do not know to try to sell things to them. This new usage is now beginning to be registered in the dictionaries.

To show how meaning is constituted in discourse, we will present one word in detail. We want to show that there is no magic formula, inside or outside of the discourse, no concept or no feature of 'reality' that we can identify as the thing the word stands for. Words are symbols. But they do not stand for something unequivocally assigned to them by some infallible deity for a shorter or longer eternity. A word in a text refers to (or is a trace of) previous occurrences of the same word, in the same text, or in all previous texts to which the present text, sometimes explicitly, but mostly implicitly, refers. It refers to all that has been said about that word previously. As we know, people do not always agree with each other. For corpus linguists, this is good news. For then we find a discussion going on in the discourse community, with various factions making different claims about what they consider to be reality. If this controversial feature can be subsumed under one concept, then each faction will try to define this concept as it suits their views. They will volunteer to present their views in the form of paraphrases of the linguistic expression in question to the linguists on silver trays.

The word we have chosen for the investigation here is *globalization* (or in its alternative spelling, *globalization*). This word is a derivation from the adjective *global*, which has been part of the English language for many centuries without changing its meaning in a noticeable way. From this adjective, it was always possible to form the word *globalization*, and, though not very frequently, it happened now and then. Not all dictionary-makers have registered that somewhere in the 1990s this word suddenly embarked on an unprecedented career. Thus, the relatively recent *NODE* has only a very short entry for *globalize*:

> **globalize** (also **-ise**) verb
> develop or be developed so as to make possible international influence or operation.

In the same entry, *globalization* is mentioned only as a derived noun, meaning nothing more than 'the process or activity of making something global'. Globalization was not always as popular as it is today. In 1983, the economic scientist Ted Levitt entitled one of his articles for the *Harvard Business Review* 'The globalization of markets'. This journal is obligatory reading for all leading experts, and Ted Levitt is a well-known figure. There are only nine sentences with the actual word *globalization* in his ten-page article. The article does not define *globalization* as a term, nor does it introduce it as a new word; rather it is used assuming everyone understands it. It seems to have been this very article that determined the current usage of *globalisation* that has made the term a household word in disciplines such as economics and social and political studies. As terms need to be defined, specialized terminological dictionaries do so, and give us a host of definitions. However, in general language lexicography, *globalization* is not recognized as a new word by a number of reference dictionaries. We have already mentioned *NODE* but we do not find *globalization* in *The Oxford Dictionary of New Words* (1997) either. The *Macmillan English Dictionary for Advanced Learners* (2002), however, tells us that *globalization* is 'the idea that the world is developing a single economy and culture as a result of improved technology and communications and the influence of very large multinational companies'.

What does the corpus tell us about the meaning of *globalization/globalisation*? First of all, it tells us that most citations in British sources of the Bank of English use the form with *s*, while almost all citations in the US part of the sources use the form with *z* (although *z* is also the preferred form for some British publishers, including Continuum, the publishers of this book). It is useful to look at them separately, because it just may happen that British *globalisation* has a meaning that differs from American *globalization*.

But before we look at this example in more detail, we will explore the notion of meaning as usage and paraphrase.

2.4 Meaning as usage and paraphrase

How does corpus linguistics deal with meaning? Meaning, as has been said before, is in the discourse. But how do we look for it there? How do we find it? There are two main aspects to meaning. Meaning is usage and paraphrase. Usage and paraphrase reflect the two ways we deal with language. We can participate in the discourse as speakers and as hearers.

Knowing the usage of a word or other lexical item lets us participate successfully in discourse. To make ourselves understood as speakers we must use linguistic items according to the expectations of hearers. These expectations are based on what has been said before. Since everybody has heard time and again the phrase 'the increasing globalisation of the financial markets', it will offend no one if we use *globalisation* with *increasing* as an adjectival modifier, and with *of the financial markets* as a genitive or prepositional modifier, depending on what you prefer to call it. There are other adjectives that often modify *globalisation*, and there are other nouns we frequently find in the genitive phrase modifiers. We also find that *globalisation* can be part of a genitive phrase modifying another noun, such as *the effects of globalisation*. This kind of contextual data determines the usage of a word. For nouns such as *globalisation*, we should also know of which verb phrases it can be the subject, and which verbs it can complement. Not all the information we find is relevant for establishing the usage of a lexical item. But the words, together with their phrasal positions, which occur with a satisfactory frequency and with a defined statistical frequency in the context of the lexical item in question (i.e. *globalisation*), make up its usage. As long as we, as discourse participants, stick to the established usage, we cannot go wrong. But once we say 'the green globalisation of our forgotten noses' we will have lost our audience. Nobody will listen to us, and we will be told we are talking nonsense. There is nothing remotely similar to this phrase in established usage that could serve as an analogy for interpreting it. Usage is something that can be established by a computer. That means in order to deal with the usage of a lexical item, we do not necessarily have to understand it, in the sense that we would be able to paraphrase it. Computers can create texts fully complying with the established usage of all the lexical items that form the text. They might be indistinguishable from texts of certain politicians, but this does not imply that the computers knew what they were saying. In this sense, usage is meaning only in a very twisted way.

Usage, however, is what we have to learn as discourse participants. It is what comes naturally to native speakers, it seems. Those who are striving to acquire English as a second language have to learn consciously that bereavement in the context of guilt is expressed by *grief*, while bereavement in the context of sadness is always felt as *sorrow*, and not the other way around. Usage is therefore something we have to cope with as members of the discourse community, as little as it may help us with the understanding of a lexical item.

Determining the usage of lexical items and coping with it are essential to the methodology of corpus linguistics. It is as close as computational methods can hope to approximate the mystery of meaning. Whenever we want the computer to identify a word as part of a unit of meaning in a corpus, it will be done through established usage. The profile of usage generated by the computer (which itself is incapable of understanding, incapable of what is sometimes called 'interpreting symbols') is like the fingerprint of a word as part of a unit of meaning: it identifies the person without telling you who the person is. The usage profile is the device in computation that can resolve ambiguity.

Meaning, we have said, is usage and paraphrase. The computer can give us the usage profile of a unit of meaning without knowing what it means. But the computer does not know and cannot know what it means. Indeed it seems as if humans are the only species of the kingdom of machines or animals who have a tendency to think about what something is about. When they see, in springtime, bees flying from blossom to blossom, they believe they know that this is about making honey, and has the additional fortuitous effect that the blossoms get fertilized. They see these two aspects as the meaning of why bees fly. The bee does not know why it is flying (and probably does not care about it). And while a computer, programmed for this task, may have no problem in translating the sentence 'Bees fly from flower to flower to produce honey' into the French sentence *'Les abeilles volent de la fleur à la fleur pour produire le miel'* (translation produced by the Altavista browser) we would not believe for a minute that this machine or the program it runs on has any idea about bees, flowers or honey. Only humans can appreciate aboutness. Only they can deal with signs. For something like flying bees is 'about' something else only when we take this something (flying bees) as a symbol for something else (producing honey). But is not the flower then a symbol for the bee signifying that it will find sugar there? I don't think it is. I don't think the bee will reason along the lines of 'oh, over there I can see (or smell) a flower – I take this to mean that I'll find sugar there'. An appreciation of aboutness presupposes consciousness, awareness. Only humans can be conscious in this sense. This unique human mental ability to find out consciously (rather than randomly) what something is about is called intentionality. In the philosophy of mind there has been a long debate about whether intentionality really is a human trait or perhaps just an illusion. If it were nothing but an illusion, then we could say the human mind is, in principle, the same as a computer, only more complex. But if intentionality exists, computers will never become like humans, and we will always be able to pull the plug when we feel like it. The issue of intentionality is very skilfully discussed in John Searle's book *Intentionality* (Searle 1983).

Only something that is a sign can mean something, because only a sign can signify something other than itself. We can say that our life has a meaning only if we take it to be a sign, a symbol for something else. Things, events, processes which we do not interpret as signs do not mean anything. However, there are different kinds of signs: symptoms, icons and symbols in the narrow sense. What we have mentioned above, the flying bees as signs that they are on their way to produce honey, is a symptom. It is something we can figure out, not because flying bees bear some resemblance to a honey jar, but because the discourse is full of stories about bees flying around to produce honey. What we did, when we saw those bees, was to remember those stories and to use our common sense to infer that they were up to honey-making. The second kind of sign are icons, signs that somehow give you a visual (or oral or tactile) clue of what they, as signs, stand for. A big picture at the roadside representing a honey pot will probably mean that there is someone there who wants to sell their honey. Icons are signs that we interpret in terms of their resemblance to whatever is indicative of some thing, act or event. Interpreting icons is, again, largely an application of common sense, together with memory of other instances to which this instance may be analogous. Finally, symbols in the narrow sense are signs to which a meaning has been assigned arbitrarily. The vocabulary of a language is commonly seen as a set of such symbols. Some people may speak as if it is the dictionary or lexicographers who assign meanings to words. But the lexicographers only document the meanings that are already assigned. It is the discourse community that assigns meanings to words (or, rather, to lexical items). Members of this community may not always be happy with the meanings they find assigned, and they are free to change the assignments, for the sign, the lexical item, does not resemble what it stands for. If, in England, the word *robin* stands for one kind of bird, that does not prevent Americans from deciding that in their variety of English the word stands for quite a different bird. It is not particularly surprising that words such as *beech*, *bream*, *grasshopper* and *magpie* have different meanings in different parts of the English-speaking world. With icons, of course, it cannot be so simple. A placard representing a jar of honey can hardly indicate that you can buy green asparagus. Flying bees will never signify that coal is being mined. A good guide to signs is Rudi Keller's book *A Theory of Linguistic Signs* (1998).

Meaning is an aspect of signs, of symptoms, icons and symbols. Meaning is one of the aspects, form being the other. Meaning and form are inseparable. Once you take away the form, the meaning vanishes. This is why it is wrong to look at language as a system into which you can encode a message and from which you can decode a message. There is no message without form. Thus it is wrong to say the text contains a meaning; the text is the meaning.

There are many theories about meaning, and almost all claim that the meaning of a linguistic unit is something outside of the discourse. Some say the meaning is what the linguistic unit refers to, out there in some discourse-external reality; others say that the meaning corresponds to some representation we have in our minds; some say meaning is represented by semantically interpreted logical calculus or some other formal system. Reality will hardly do, as we have pointed out above. It is, before it is ordered and structured by language, amorphous and chaotic. Mental representations only multiply our problems. For either these representations are also signs, in which case their meaning is inseparable from their form, and to get at their meaning, we would have to come up with yet another representation, and

85

still another one on top of that, and so on. (John Searle, in his book *The Rediscovery of the Mind*, 1992, refers to this phenomenon as the 'homunculus' problem, while for Daniel Dennett, in his book *Consciousness Explained*, 1993, it is the problem of the 'central meaner'. Both scholars agree that translating the meaning of a linguistic unit into a mental representation is nothing but a fallacy.) Or, if mental representations are translations of meaning into an expression of some formal system, we are still no better off. For how would we know what the expressions of such a formal system mean? We could only explain them in natural language, and then we are back at square one. Of course we can translate any sentence or text into an artificial language such as Esperanto. But to understand that Esperanto sentence or text we would have to re-translate it into a language we are familiar with. We just cannot escape the prison of natural language. All these attempts to approach meaning are like burning wood in a stove: if we succeed, we are left with nothing. Once the form has burned, the meaning has vanished.

Our point of departure was that a sign is something that stands for something else. But if, as we have been arguing, it does not stand for something in some reality not affected by the discourse, if it does not stand for a representation in the mind, if it does not stand for some expression in a formal linguistic system, then what does it stand for? When you are asked what a cantaloupe is, or a unicorn, what comes to your mind? You may remember market stalls where you have seen heaps of cantaloupes, you may remember eating cantaloupe, and the taste and texture of the fruit perhaps come to your mind. You may remember stories you were told about unicorns, or you may have read about them. You may also remember what you have told other people about them. You may remember a picture in a children's book, or a Burgundian wall-hanging, or a little illustration in a medieval manuscript, depicting a unicorn. Isn't that what meaning is, what the linguistic signs *cantaloupe* and *unicorn* stand for?

If we were to take these memories to be the meaning of lexical units, then we would adopt the position of cognitive linguistics. Our mental representations would not be as orderly as Anna Wierzbicka (1996) would like them to be, and certainly these representations would not be anything like universal, because everyone's memories are unique, and they would contain ineffable qualia like your or my taste experience of cantaloupes. Your memories form your understanding of cantaloupes and unicorns, and they would be reflected in your response to the question of what these items are. But these memories are private and individual, and therefore they cannot be the meaning of the signs *cantaloupe* and *unicorn*.

Language is a social, not a psychological phenomenon, and so is meaning. The meaning of *cantaloupe* and *unicorn* is what is said about them in the discourse. Your response to the question of what these items are will be a new contribution to the discourse, and it may well contain statements that have not been said before. If your audience is happy with them, they may remember them, and they may even repeat them in suitable situations. In ten or twenty years, you might even find traces of it in new editions of dictionaries. On the other hand, your audience will also compare what you say with what they have heard before. If what you say disagrees with their memories, they will ask other members of the discourse community. Unless they quote from dictionaries, it is highly improbable that those who volunteer their view of cantaloupes and unicorns will repeat anyone else's statements *verbatim*, word for word. If your audience is still unsatisfied with what they are being told, they might resort to querying libraries, archives and even the Internet. In the end, they will come up with a host of reports on cantaloupes and on unicorns. Some of these reports look more or less like definitions; some like more technical explanations; many are just stories. A lot will overlap each other, while some reports will not be supported by any others. There could be a lot of disagreement. Should we trust Caesar when he claims there were real unicorns in the Teutonic forests, for example? Many of the statements will in fact not be directly about cantaloupes and unicorns but about what other people have said about them, about how reliable or credible their claims are.

We call all these statements, definitions, explanations and stories that focus on cantaloupes or on unicorns, paraphrases. What all the paraphrases of the word *unicorn* will definitely have in common is that they paraphrase the word *unicorn*. That alone is what keeps them together. Otherwise they may be as different as they come. This set of paraphrases, then, is the meaning of the lexical item *unicorn*. It cannot be reduced to a simple formula. It is fuzzy, vague, full of contradictions; some of it may be true and some of it may be wrong. It is not the linguist's task to filter out what they think is right. This is what the linguistic sign *unicorn* stands for: the set of paraphrases dealing with unicorns. This is what the word *unicorn* is about.

Meaning as paraphrase thus shows us another way of identifying units of meaning. In this perspective, a unit of meaning is whatever we find paraphrases for in the discourse. Usage profiles can be handled efficiently by computers. Paraphrases, on the other hand, have to be interpreted. They have to be understood. This is something computers cannot do. Therefore they will never know what cantaloupes and unicorns are.

After these rather lengthy remarks about usage and paraphrase, we can finally return to the case study of the meaning of the word *globalization*. In the following section, we show how a computer can create a usage profile for us.

2.5 Globalization

To start, we have analysed a sample of 200 citations (from the Bank of English) of *globalisation*, and asked the computer to give us the most frequent collocates of the word. Among the most frequent collocates are the following words: *anti*, *world*, *against*, *means*, *economic*, *international* and *business*, as illustrated by the following concordance lines:

```
        Forum, the main anti- globalisation umbrella group at the
      defended against anti- globalisation protesters by one of
    than we used to. Despite globalisation, the world has at the
      debate, related to the globalisation of the world economy,
      of the protest against globalisation is, however, mistakenly
         has held our against globalisation of culture for a long time
       is the argument that globalisation means economic problems
   artistic strategies. Globalisation here means the same old
            and economic globalisation was kidding themselves
   economic policy is the globalisation of markets. If economic
     change in the wake of globalisation, international competi-
     related has been the globalisation of international manu-
            in business law globalisation will cause even worse
   illogical attacks on the globalisation of business
```

As we have said before, it is useful in this case to look separately at the spelling variant with *z* in order to establish whether *globalization* is used differently. Already the total number of actual occurrences in the Bank of English is quite different: *globalization* occurs 468 times, while the total number of the citations for *globalisation* is 1,447. This can be easily explained by the fact that the data in the Bank of English are 'biased' towards British English in which the spelling with *s* is more common. But that is not the whole truth. If we look at the sources of the citations, we can see that citations for *globalisation* come mainly from newspaper texts and citations for *globalization* are mainly from books, many of them American (but also some British). The most frequent collocates for *globalization* (based on a sample of 200) are only partly the same as above. We do find such collocates as: *economic, markets, world, investment, financial, international* but we do not find *anti* or *against*.

To find some of the paraphrases of *globalisation* we looked up a sample of what the corpus tells us about 'what globalisation is':

```
          degradation. But globalisation is a fact and, by
     rapidly changing world. Globalisation is a much overused word
       on the world stage.'' Globalisation is a trend that many
       technological change. Globalisation is a catch-all to
        and access to capital. Globalisation is a redistribution
       conventional wisdom on globalisation is a relic of the
    war and the economics of globalisation is a story which gets
         the poor even poorer. Globalisation is a fancy euphemism
        problem in particular. Globalisation is a market-led process,
          in inverted commas. Globalisation is a term that Giddens
           at Conduit, explains: 'Globalisation is a trend that everyone
            major issues. Still, globalisation is a process that has
            you realise that globalisation is an accepted phenomenon
     and benefiting from, globalisation is an open society, in
          may be in danger. Globalisation is an opportunity and a
        apreciation is that globalisation is an unstoppable force,
   lot of the criticism of globalisation is based on ignorance
           Mr Rubin argues globalisation is both good and inevi-
      Precisely because globalisation'' is demonised as an
       Etzioni argue that globalisation is destroying communities
       euro's arrival is that globalisation is here to stay as
        the allegation that globalisation is inherently harmful.
      those who say that globalisation is just a bigger market,
        - with mixed results. Globalisation is like a giant wave,
      The reality is that globalisation is not inevitable, it is
    tourists. All the same, globalisation is not to be resisted,
      best way to deal with globalisation is not to fight it but
             however, that globalisation is not a painless exercise
   trend towards increasing globalisation is not easily
        past few months show, globalisation is not a one-way street.
     must demonstrate that globalisation is not just a code word
        a sounder basis for globalisation is required. If neither
    voiced an anxiety that globalisation is robbing nations
```

```
    left in the age of globalisation is tearing apart even
    the global economy. Globalisation is the big issue of our
  humbly born. To be anti- globalisation is to march, under the
```

As we can see, globalization 'is' and 'is not' lots of things. The discourse takes notice of the fact that, if there is a relationship between the word *globalisation* and some discourse-external reality, it is not an easy one. We are told that *globalisation* is a much overused word, a story, a fancy euphemism, a term, and not just a code word or a one-way street. This shows how we can use natural language to talk about language. It is something we cannot do in formal languages like mathematics, logical calculi, or programming languages. There you have to move outside the system to be able to talk about it. But where should we move from our language? Indeed every other language, every formal language, can be defined only by natural language. There is no formal algorithm, no calculus that would not need this kind of definition or explanation in a natural language. And therefore we have to use our own language to discuss it. If we look at the context left to *globalisation*, we see that people discuss the way in which other people use *globalisation*. Someone explains, you realize, there is an appreciation and also a criticism, people argue, demonstrate or say that *globalisation* is this or that.

But what is the thing behind the word? Globalization is: a fact, a trend, a process, a phenomenon, an opportunity, an unstoppable force; it is both good and inevitable; is here to stay; is inherently harmful; is like a giant wave; is not inevitable; is not to be resisted; is not a painless exercise; and is the big issue. This looks confusing. Is it not inevitable, or is it here to stay? Is it harmful, or is it good? For whom is it an opportunity, for whom is it a painful exercise? Can we understand the word on the basis of these citations? Can we define it?

Our corpus is the Bank of English, with about 450 million words. The texts it contains were spoken or written mainly in the last 20 years and it is strongly biased towards British English. When we go through the concordance lines of *globalisation* we notice there is a lot of debating, worrying and talking about globalization; there are many protests, demonstrations and campaigns against globalization, and we find many instances of anti-globalization and anti-globalization protesters; globalization is economic and increasing, there is an ongoing globalization process; people talk about an age or era of globalization, about the benefits, the challenge, the impact, the pressures, the forces and effects of globalisation. This all sounds familiar. Globalization is often also connected with emotions, and these are predominantly negative ones. About one-third of the citations are of neutral tone and only about one-tenth of them can be considered to have a positive tone. This occurs mainly in the context of business, politics and new technology.

We get a slightly different picture if we look at *globalization*. Not all of these instances are American English, for the *OED* prefers the spelling with *z*. Here is a sample of the citations:

```
    the impact of economic globalization on the world of work
overwhelmed by the rapid globalization of economic
    trends, including the globalization of markets.
  us a picture of how this globalization of financial markets
  elsewhere in the world, globalization holds the promise of
  This is the world of new globalization of borders easily
    itself a result of the globalization of investment. While
  illustrates cost of the globalization of investment. It also
technology and increasing globalization challenging the way
    Third, there has been a globalization of the international
        In this new form of globalization, the international
```

The most apparent differences from the previous citations are the matter-of-fact tone and the different genre from which these citations come.

Let's compare our corpus evidence with Ted Levitt's use of the word *globalization* in 1983. The following are the citations from his article:

> The **globalization** of markets is at hand.

> Nor is the sweeping gale of **globalization** confined to these raw material or high-tech products, where the universal language of customers and users facilitates standardization.

> The theory holds, at this stage in the evolution of **globalization**, no matter what conventional market research and even common sense may suggest about different national and regional tastes, preferences, needs, and institutions.

> Barriers to **globalization** are not confined to the Middle East.

> It orchestrates the twin vectors of technology and **globalization** for the world's benefit.

> The differences that persist throughout the world despite its **globalization** affirm an ancient dictum of economics – that things are driven by what happens at the margin, not at the core.

> To refer to the persistence of economic nationalism (protective and subsidized trade practices, special tax aids, or restrictions for home producers) as a barrier to the **globalization** of markets is to make a valid point.

> Two vectors shape the world – technology and **globalization**.

> Given what is everywhere the purpose of commerce, the global company will shape the vectors of technology and **globalization** into its great strategic fecundity.

Levitt's first use of the word *globalization* in his article (apart from the title) is in the following sentence: *The globalization of markets is at hand*. In the Bank of English there are eleven occurrences of *globalisation of markets* and five of *globalization of markets* as illustrated by the following lines:

```
of stocks. Also, as globalisation of markets continues to
a mystery where the globalisation of markets is taking us. Its
  adjustment to the globalisation of markets and the influence
    into account the globalisation of markets and of the features
      because of the globalisation of markets, which will have
        rapidly with globalisation of markets. Kevin Bales reports
```

Levitt talks about 'the globalization of markets' being 'at hand'. All the evidence from the Bank of English shows that 'globalisation of markets' is now an established notion. It tells us what is happening with the 'globalisation of markets' presently: it 'grows' and we have to take it 'into account'.

Levitt mentions *globalization* for the second time when he talks about how 'globalization' influences world business; the expression he uses is the 'gale of globalization'. In the Bank of English we find no occurrences of 'gale of globalisation'. If we look up what comes as a 'gale of', we find it is mostly 'giggles' and 'laughter' and 'wind', but we do also find *gale of economic change, energy* or *modernity*, notions closely related to globalization.

The third occurrence of *globalization* in Levitt's text is in the phrase 'the evolution of globalization', which has no occurrences in our corpus. This may correspond to our earlier finding that 'globalisation' in our contemporary language use is an established notion. Levitt mentions 'barriers to globalization' twice in his text. There are no citations for exactly the same wording in our corpus, but if we look up 'barriers to' we can see that most frequently we talk about 'barriers to entry' and *barriers to trade*, again facts closely related with globalisation. Levitt strongly associates *technology and globalization* (three occurrences in his text); and indeed, judging from the evidence from Bank of English, globalisation is still very much associated with technology both directly and indirectly.

```
 pressure from technology and globalisation 'the half-life
benefit from new technology and globalisation than others,
arthritic. When technology and globalisation demanded changes
   INFORMATION technology and globalisation are the driving
  arguing that technology and globalisation are tending to
  of clothes. Technology and globalisation mean that every-
 the impact of technology and globalisation, where business
       needs. Technology and globalisation have revolu-
Why? 'Because of technology and globalization, everyone has
```

The last occurrence of *globalization* in Levitt's text is the following:

The differences that persist throughout the world despite its globalization affirm an ancient dictum of economics – that things are driven by what happens at the margin, not at the core.

A search for *globalisation* and *despite* yielded the following lines:

```
        insular despite the globalisation that affects
   But, despite all of this, globalisation has been the source
despite the drift towards globalisation, national policies
   despite the increasing globalisation of the capital
       despite pressures of globalisation, it will take a
```

What we present here is based on insufficient evidence. We do not know if there are differences between American and British usage, as we do not have a comparable corpus of American English. Our citations are not classified according to domain, genre, text type or publication date. We cannot see if there was a change of meaning, and we do not know whether *globalisation* is used differently in texts written for the public at large from texts addressed at a professional audience. The structure of the Bank of English makes it hard to extract the information needed for this kind of classification. But the evidence we have for example clearly suggests there is a difference in tone, depending on the genre: texts from newspapers often have a sceptical tone, while the tone of professional and academic writing is more 'matter of fact'. This is not surprising; in fact it could have been expected and it is most probably also true of many other words.

This, then, is how and what corpus linguistics can contribute to the meaning of the word *globalization/globalisation*. It is the evidence of the corpus citations of *globalization/globalisation* within their contexts, condensed and brought into some kind of contingent order. It is much more than we would find in any dictionary, and, at the same time, it does not have the coherence of an encyclopaedic article. It is obviously in many points contradictory; it is nothing like a definition. Is this the meaning of *globalization*? Globalization has become such an important fact of our society that social scientists have felt the need to define it. 'Globalization' has thus established itself as a term. Let's have a look at its complex definition in the *Oxford Dictionary of Sociology* (1998). Is it so very different from some of our citations?

globalization, globalization theory

Globalization theory examines the emergence of a global cultural system. It suggests that global culture is brought about by a variety of social and cultural developments: the existence of a world-satellite information system; the emergence of global patterns of consumption and consumerism; the cultivation of cosmopolitan life-styles; the emergence of global sport such as the Olympic Games ... the spread of world tourism; the decline of the sovereignty of the nation-state ... More importantly, globalism involves a new consciousness of the world as a single place. ... Perhaps the most concise definition suggests that globalization is 'a social process in which the constraints of geography on social and cultural arrangements recede and in which people are becoming increasingly aware that they are receding' (Malcolm Waters, Globalization, 1995) ... Contemporary globalization theory argues that globalization comprises two entirely contradictory processes of homogenization and differentiation; and that there are powerful movements of resistance against globalization processes ... It is undoubtedly true that, on a planet in which the same fashion accessories (such as designer training-shoes) are manufactured and sold across every continent, one can send and receive electronic mail from the middle of a forest in Brazil, eat McDonald's hamburgers in Moscow as well as Manchester, and pay for all this using a Mastercard linked to a bank account in Madras, then the world does indeed appear to be increasingly 'globalized'. However, the excessive use of this term as a sociological buzzword has largely emptied it of analytical and explanatory value...

As globalization is a worldwide phenomenon, we need not restrict ourselves to the English-language evidence. There are also some interesting data available about *Globalisierung*, its German equivalent, based on the analysis of one single newspaper, the *Tageszeitung*. It was only in the year 1996 that *Globalisierung* gained ground. From 1988 until the end of 1995 we find altogether about 160 citations. Then, suddenly, for the year 1996 the figure jumps up to 320, and from then on remains more or less on the same level. Before 1996, *Globalisierung* was used as an *ad hoc* formation derived from *global*, without any specific meaning other than 'the action or process of something turning global'. In each instance, it was necessary to specify what was being globalized, and therefore *Globalisierung* never came alone, but was always in the company of modifiers (such as in *die Globalisierung der modernen Lebensweise*, the globalization of the modern way of life). For the year 1996, when the word suddenly made a jump in frequency (indicating, among other things, that a change of meaning, from something more general to something more specific, had occurred), we find a large number of citations in which *Globalisierung* comes without modifiers, but with explanations or paraphrases (*in der Tat bedeutet Globalisierung Amerikanisierung*, indeed, globalization means Americanization). By the time that everyone is supposed to understand what *Globalisierung* means, this percentage goes down again, and we find again many modifiers. Before 1996, the modifiers appeared to be a random lot – everything could be connected to *Globalisierung*. After 1996, the same modifiers recurred time and again; the new meaning of *Globalisierung* associated the word mostly with finance, trade, technology, the economy at large, and the workforce, indeed remarkably similar to the modifiers we find with *globalisation/globalization* in the Bank of English.

We deliberately chose the word *globalisation/globalization* as a neologism. Must we not assume that all words once were neologisms? Before Lucullus brought the cherry (*cerasus*) from Persia to Rome, there was no need for a name for it. It makes sense to assume that the introduction of neologisms into the discourse always occurs along the same lines. As long as the word (or larger unit of meaning) is still new, it needs to be explained. Not everyone understands the word in the same way. Explanations also serve the purpose of negotiating the meaning of a word within the discourse community. It can take a while before the larger part of the audience has come to some kind of tacit agreement. From then on, only those discourse participants who object to the agreement will come up with new paraphrases. In principle, we can say that once the meaning of a new word has become uncontroversial it can be used to paraphrase other units of meaning.

The word *globalization* shows nicely that the discourse community is not at all homogenous. The discourse community is, it should be remembered, identical with the society whose language we are dealing with, and it is as multifaceted as this society is. So while for one section of the discourse community the meaning of *globalization* has become established and accepted, there are other sections still in disagreement. This is why the paraphrases and explanations we find in the corpus do not have a common denominator and why, at times, they even contradict each other. Contradictory evidence, however, is not what we have come to regard, in traditional lexicography, as the meaning of a word. Now, once we have presented the citations, we must sift the evidence and write up a coherent, concise definition that we can put into the dictionary. Now we must find the magic formula.

There is no secret formula; and there is no overt formula, unless we leave it to a committee of experts (on what?) to define *globalization* once and for all, so that anyone who thereafter uses *globalization* differently will be reprimanded. But if this were to happen, *globalization* would have ceased to be a natural language word; it would have become a term in a formal system of terminology. Corpus linguistics has nothing to contribute to standardized terminology. No contribution to the discourse will ever change the meaning of a standardized term, because it has no meaning other than the definition assigned to it. *Ascorbic acid, DNA* or *electrolytic rectifier* are terms with relatively fixed meaning, hardly variable in any imaginable context.

Why do new words occur? Why do other words disappear? Will *globaloney* be as widely used in 20 years' time as *globalization* is today? In December 2002 *Newsweek* published an article 'The new buzzword: globaloney'. The article begins: 'So far as we can tell, congresswoman Clare Boothe Luce coined the term "globaloney" in 1943 to trash what Vice President Henry Wallace liked to call his "global thinking" ...' (Miller 2002).

There are only five citations for *globaloney* in the Bank of English and they all are from British sources.

```
          in impressive-sounding globaloney are provided by
and more earlier. For all the globaloney to be found in modern
    LSE lecture last week - is globaloney. Much of the talk about
 nosed divi, talkin a load o' globaloney (Fings ain' t what they
         Business, 1993. Hirst, P. Globaloney in Prospect,
```

It is only recently that *globaloney*, as in the example below from the *Mail on Sunday* (22 July 2001), has started appearing more frequently in the press as a reaction to the phenomenon of globalization. We have to wait to see whether it catches on.

> These 'anti-globalist' demonstrators are globalists themselves. Whether they are hippy-dippy groups concerned with peace, the environment and Third World debt, or old-fashioned leftie groups with a tradition of small-scale violence, they all want to replace the present globalisation with their own form of globaloney.

Words are different from terms. A word we find in the text resonates with an infinite number of previous citations, many of them shared between the speaker and the hearer, because they have grown up in the same discourse community and have been exposed to many of the same texts. It is in the light of these previous citations that the speaker uses the word and that the hearer will understand it. It is linguists who define the discourse community. They decide how deeply they want to dig into the past, and they define where the lines are drawn at the fringes. But even given these limitations, this discourse is just not available *in toto*, neither to the linguists nor to any members of the discourse community. None of them will ever be able to capture the full meaning of a word (or a larger unit of meaning). When we read or listen to texts we have not previously encountered, we may well be confronted with citations showing new semantic aspects. What we find out about the meaning of a word will never be more than an approximation.

2.6 What corpus linguistics can tell us about the meaning of words

In 1976, a relatively unknown author by the name of Courtlandt D. B. Bryan writes a novel about an American soldier in Vietnam killed accidentally by fire from American forces, and he calls this novel *Friendly Fire*. This phrase immediately catches on, and now, also due to two wars against Iraq, there is hardly anyone left in the English-speaking world who does not know what *friendly fire* means. During the last war against Iraq, journalists started using more widely another expression for 'friendly fire': *blue on blue*. During the war, the *Guardian* featured a series of articles on 'The language of war'. *Blue on blue* had an entry of its own explaining its meaning and origin:

> Blue on blue, which made its debut yesterday after the downing of an RAF Tornado by an American Patriot missile, comes from wargaming exercises where the goodies are blue and – in a hangover from cold war days – the baddies are red. Replaces the

older term 'friendly fire' which, as Murphy's Laws of
Combat eloquently note, isn't.
(Stuart Millar, *Guardian*, 24 March 2003)

This is nothing that could have been predicted by linguists. As we have seen for *globalization*, there is no rule
that can predict the emergence of new expressions. And
there is no rule which tells us whether an expression will
catch on or not. *Friendly fire* is a fairly recent addition to
our vocabulary. The title of this 1976 novel quickly
entered the general discourse. It replaced the military
term *fratricide*, which we also find in French. But *fratricide* is a word meaning 'the killing of one's brother (or
sister)'. As such, it is rare and smacks of erudition.
Friendly fire, on the other hand, has a familiar ring, in
spite of being a neologism. With each subsequent war, it
became more popular. In the 450 million words of the
Bank of English, there are 267 occurrences of this phrase.
Here are a few citations:

```
      those men died from friendly fire, a phenomenon which he said
      Author C.D.F. Bryan < Friendly Fire> came to the five-day
   may have been killed in friendly fire. General Johnston also said
         Relatives of the friendly fire victims are angrily accusing
      mistakes, accidents 'friendly fire', including Private Errol
```

Do lexicographers regard *friendly fire* as a unit of meaning? The largest online English dictionary is WordNet, an
electronic database that has been compiled for some
years now – and is still being compiled – at Princeton
University under the guidance of Christiane Fellbaum.
WordNet is more than a traditional dictionary. It systematically lists relations between each entry and other
entries, such as synonymy, hyponymy, meronymy and
antonymy. It organizes the senses which it assigns to its
entries as 'synsets' (sets of synonyms), where each synset
is defined as a list of all entries sharing this particular
meaning. All synsets or senses come with glosses and

often also with an example. For several years now, WordNet has been listing collocations as well. But we did not find an entry for *friendly fire*. There could have been several possible reasons. The phrase was too new, or it was not frequent enough, or it was thought not to be a unit of meaning. The third of these reasons turned out to be the case.

The adjective *friendly* has four senses in WordNet:

1. friendly (vs. unfriendly) – (characteristic of or befitting a friend; 'friendly advice'; 'a friendly neighborhood'; 'the only friendly person here'; 'a friendly host and hostess')
2. friendly – (favorably disposed; not antagonistic or hostile; 'a government friendly to our interests'; 'an amicable agreement')
3. friendly (vs. unfriendly) – ((in combination) easy to understand or use; 'user-friendly computers'; 'a consumer-friendly policy'; 'a reader-friendly novel')
4. friendly (vs. hostile) – (of or belonging to your own country's forces or those of an ally; 'in friendly territory'; 'he was accidentally killed by friendly fire')

This entry shows that a deliberate decision was made not to enter *friendly fire* as a collocation. For the compilers of WordNet, the phrase is a combination of two units of meaning. Are they right? Is there a separate sense of *friendly* accounting for cases such as *friendly fire* and *friendly territory*? Are there other phrases where we find this sense of *friendly*, such as *friendly houses, friendly planes, friendly newspapers*? Friendly houses seems to belong to synset 1 (cf. *friendly neighbourhood*), *friendly newspapers* seems to belong to synset 2 ('favourably disposed'). So perhaps there are really only two instances for the fourth synset. The antonym of *friendly territory*

103

(Google: ca 6,500,000 hits) is sometimes *hostile territory* (Google: ca 1,100,000 hits), but more often *enemy territory* (Google: ca 2,970,000 hits). The antonym of *friendly fire* (Google: ca 51,200,000 hits) is sometimes *hostile fire* (Google: 1,380,000 hits), but again more often *enemy fire* (15,600,000 hits). Both antonyms should be mentioned in the entry. The question is whether it makes sense to construe a sense that is limited to two instances.

Let us now have a look at *fire* in WordNet. The noun *fire* has eight senses in WordNet.

1. fire – (the event of something burning (often destructive); 'they lost everything in the fire')
2. fire, flame, flaming – (the process of combustion of inflammable materials producing heat and light and (often) smoke; 'fire was one of our ancestors' first discoveries')
3. fire, firing – (the act of firing weapons or artillery at an enemy; 'hold your fire until you can see the whites of their eyes'; 'they retreated in the face of withering enemy fire')
4. fire – (a fireplace in which a fire is burning; 'they sat by the fire and talked')
5. fire, attack, flak, flack, blast – (intense adverse criticism; 'Clinton directed his fire at the Republican Party'; 'the government has come under attack'; 'don't give me any flak')
6. ardor, ardour, fervor, fervour, fervency, fire, fervidness – (feelings of great warmth and intensity; 'he spoke with great ardor')
7. fire – ((archaic) once thought to be one of four elements composing the universe (Empedocles))
8. fire – (a severe trial; 'he went through fire and damnation')

The sense we are interested in is, of course, sense 3. Here we find the phrase *enemy fire* in an example. Adding up the glosses for sense 4 of *friendly* and sense 3 of *fire*, we obtain, *mutatis mutandis*, 'the act of firing weapons ... at our own or our allies' forces'. This is an appropriate definition. Is WordNet right to deny *friendly fire* the status of a unit of meaning? While other dictionaries have nothing equivalent to WordNet sense 4 of *friendly*, some of them list *friendly fire* as a separate entry, recognizing the phrase as a unit of meaning, e.g. *NODE*: [Military] 'weapon fire coming from one's own side that causes accidental injury or death to one's own people'. Both options seem legitimate. The disadvantage of the first alternative is that it introduces a polysemy which does not exist if we accept the unit of meaning as a solution. In the context of *fire*, *friendly* can only mean sense 4, and in the context of *friendly*, *fire* can only mean sense 3. But multiplying the four senses of *friendly* with the eight senses of *fire*, we end up with 32 combinations, out of which we have to select the only one possible. So, if we accept Ockham's razor as the underlying principle for constructing a semantic model ('Entities are not to be multiplied without necessity'), the interpretation of *friendly fire* as a unit of meaning is obviously preferable.

From a methodological point of view, it makes sense to put *friendly fire* down as a unit of meaning because it simplifies the linguist's task to account for what a text, a sentence, a phrase mean. It is more convenient to treat the phrase as a collocation than to describe it as the contingent co-occurrence of two single words. This aspect is particularly important for the computational processing of natural language – for example, for machine translation. Computers do not ask whether the meaning of *friendly fire* (or of *false dawn*) (see 1.3) is something that cannot be inferred from the meaning of the parts they are constituted of. We use computers that do not understand what people talk about. We want them to facilitate the translation of sentences in which we encounter these and comparable phrases. The above meaning has been discussed in terms of usage and of paraphrase. Usage is something computers can cope with. If *friendly fire* is used in a unique way and not in any of the other 31 ways suggested by WordNet, then it is simpler to deal with it as a unit in its own right, as a lexical item that just happens to be composed of two words. But usage does not tell us how we understand the phrase. When we want to communicate with other members of the discourse community about how we understand *friendly fire*, we have to paraphrase it. Whether a given paraphrase, i.e. the interpretation of a phrase, is acceptable to the discourse community has to be left to the members of that community.

The question is, therefore, whether *friendly fire* is a unit of meaning also from the perspective of meaning as paraphrase. The answer to this question is simple. It is a unit of meaning if we find paraphrases telling us how others understand it, and thus, how we would do better to understand it as well. In the *NODE*, we have already found one paraphrase. That this is more than the concoction of an assiduous lexicographer is confirmed by a glance at the Bank of English. Among the citations of *friendly fire*, there are about a dozen that comment on the phrase, try to explain it, circumscribe it or downright paraphrase it, for example:

> The United States Defence Department says an investigation has shown that about one out of every four Americans killed in battle during the Gulf War died as a result of **'friendly fire'** – in other words, they were killed by their own side.

> Whether called fratricide, amicicide, blue on blue, **friendly fire**, or – as in official U.S. casualty reports from Vietnam – 'misadventure', the phenomenon had become all too commonplace on twentieth-century battlefields.

> In Vietnam, the Americans coined the phrase **'friendly fire'**, a monstrous use of the language, as if any such fire could be regarded as friendly.

> And the other problem, low visibility increases the risk of **friendly fire** – a term that means mistakenly shooting at your own side.

We learn that friendly fire is a 'phrase', a 'term', that it constitutes a 'monstrous use of language', that the Americans introduced it into the discourse in their Vietnam war, and that it means your troops are 'killed by their own side'. Paraphrases of this kind abound when a new unit of meaning, be it a single word or a collocation, enters the discourse. Then people must be told about it. As we have seen, the first evidence of *friendly fire* is probably the title of the 1976 novel. Unfortunately there are no corpora that could verify an assumption that, during that and the subsequent year, there was an abundance of paraphrases. Here again, a bilingual perspective might prove useful. What happens when translators are confronted with a lexical item for which they cannot find a translation equivalent because it has not been translated before?

Corpus linguistics tells us that translation equivalence is not something that latently always exists and just has to be discovered. Translation equivalence has to be construed. As with meaning, this construal is a communal activity, only it does not involve a discourse community of a specific language such as English, but the community of bilingual speakers of the two languages involved. One translator will come up with a proposal, which is then negotiated with the other members of that community, until agreement is reached and every translator starts using the same equivalent, or until several equivalents are considered acceptable and translators choose among them. It seems as if in the case of *friendly fire* translators had to start from scratch. Apparently there was never a fixed expression in German as an equivalent of *fratricide, blue on blue* or *friendly fire.*

Friendly fire is a phrase which is worth looking at from a bilingual perspective. What does the bilingual perspective add to the issue? This relatively new expression became more frequent only in the course of the first Gulf war, when more British soldiers were killed by friendly (mostly American) fire than by enemy fire. It was only then that the phrase began to be translated into other languages, German among them. How was it translated?

The second edition of the *Oxford–Duden*, published in 1999, acknowledges *friendly fire* as a single lexical item and gives it a separate entry. The translation equivalent it proposes is *eigenes Feuer* ('own fire'). Other translation equivalents which we find in Google and in various corpora are *freundliches Feuer, befreundetes Feuer* and the English collocation *friendly fire*, as a borrowing into German. Most of the texts we find there are texts originally written in German, not translations from the English. Still we have to assume that the concept 'friendly fire' did not exist before it was introduced into the German discourse via translations. For neither of the German equivalents mentioned above occur in the older texts of our corpora. Thus all four German options have to be seen as the results of translations.

It is noteworthy that there is, in Google, only one occurrence of *durch befreundetes Feuer* ('through/by fire of our friends'). We might have expected more, given that *befreundet* is the standard translation for the fourth meaning of *friendly* in WordNet, where we find *friendly fire* together with *friendly territory*. Indeed, *friendly territory* is *befreundetes Territorium* in German. This is a first indication that translators understand *friendly fire* as a collocation and not as a contingent combination of two single words. We can be sure that *befreundetes Feuer* will never become the default equivalent of *friendly fire*. For the phrase *durch freundliches Feuer* we find 87,300 occurrences in Google. This is a second indication that translators see *friendly fire* as a true collocation. For *freundliches Feuer* (*freundlich* being the default translation of *friendly*) would normally – without English influence – never mean 'soldiers killed by their own side' but something quite different, as in this singular Google citation:

> *Ihre nachtschwarzen Augen leuchteten jedoch in freundlichem Feuer, als sie in die Runde ihrer Amazonenkriegerinnen sah.* ('Yet her nightblack eyes glowed in a friendly fire, as she was glancing at the round of her Amazon warriors.')

As a single lexical item, as a unit of meaning, however, *freundliches Feuer* can mean anything the discourse community accepts. Before this can happen, however, people have to do a lot of explaining. This becomes evident from the two examples taken from Google:

> *Es gab 120 Verletzte durch 'freundliches Feuer' – also Treffer durch die eigenen Leute.* ('There were 120 wounded from "friendly fire" – i.e. hits by one's own people.')

> *Natürlich haben die amerikanischen Militärs auch einige elektronische Mittel erfunden, um den 'Fratrizid', wie der Tod durch 'freundliches Feuer' im offiziellen Jargon auch genannt wird, möglichst auszuschließen.* ('Of course, the American military have invented some electronic gadgets to rule out "fratricide", as death by "friendly fire" is often called in official jargon.')

In the first example the audience is told explicitly, in the form of a paraphrase, what *friendly fire* means. In both instances we find *freundliches Feuer* in quotation marks, making the audience aware that it is a new expression, and that this expression has to be understood as a unit of meaning. The next few years will show whether *freundliches Feuer* will become the default translation of *friendly fire*.

More frequent is *eigenes Feuer*, with ca 945,000 hits in Google for the phrase *durch eigenes Feuer* ('through/by own fire'). Two examples are presented which show that this phrase is the result of English interference:

> *Das Verteidigungsministerium in London hat Berichte bestätigt, nach denen durch 'eigenes Feuer' in der Nähe von Basra ein britischer Soldat getötet und fünf weitere verletzt worden sind.* ('The Ministry of Defence in London has confirmed reports that near Basra one British soldier was killed and five more were wounded by "friendly fire"'.)

> *Man kann es sich leicht vorstellen, dass es für die Moral eines militärischen Verbandes die schlimmste Erfahrung ist, wenn ein Kamerad durch eigenes Feuer, durch friendly fire, ums Leben kommt.* ('It is easy to imagine that it is the worst experience for the morale of a military unit when a comrade dies from one's own fire, from *friendly fire*.')

It seems strange indeed that the expression *eigenes Feuer*, which is very easy to understand, is put in quotation marks, but it shows that the speaker uses it as a translation of *friendly fire*. This becomes even more evident in the second example where the perfectly transparent *eigenes Feuer* is paraphrased by the much less familiar *friendly fire*. There seems to be a certain uneasiness to represent the concept expressed in English by a single unit of meaning, by a decomposable adjective+noun phrase, i.e. by two separate words. Therefore it is still doubtful whether *eigenes Feuer* will become the German default equivalent. Even though it seems to be more common, its other disadvantage is that it sounds less like *friendly fire* than the option *freundliches Feuer*.

However, the most frequent equivalent we find is the borrowing *friendly fire*. There are, in Google, ca 233,000 hits for '*durch friendly fire*'. Again we notice that in most citations, the collocation is put into quotation marks, indicating the novelty and strangeness of the expression. Here are two examples from the Österreichisches Zeitungskorpus (ÖZK; 'Austrian Newspaper Corpus'), a 500-million-word corpus covering the 1990s:

> *Und fast schon ans Zynische grenzt jene Bezeichnung, welche die Militärsprache für den irrtümlichen Beschuß der eigenen Leute kennt. Man nennt das friendly fire – freundliches Feuer.* ('And that name borders almost on cynicism which military jargon uses for mistaken fire on one's own people. They call it friendly fire – *freundliches Feuer*.')

> *An dieser Frontlinie beobachten wir auch immer wieder das, was die Militaristen 'friendly fire' nennen, nämlich Verluste in den eigenen Reihen durch fehlgeleitete Geschosse aus den eigenen, nachfolgenden Linien. Was die Haider-Diskussion anlangt, hat sich dieses Phänomen sogar zu einer Art intellektueller Selbstschußanlage verfestigt.* ('At this frontline, we keep seeing what the military call "friendly fire", i.e. losses in one's own lines from badly aimed shots from one's own rear lines. As for the discussion about Mr Haider, this phenomenon has become firmly established as a kind of intellectual automatic firing device.')

Paraphrases reveal whether a phrase has become a fixed expression, a collocation, a unit of meaning. The paraphrases in these two examples do not tell us what *friendly* means, they explain what *friendly fire* is. While we have learned above to establish, whenever expedient, collocations or fixed expressions on the basis of usage, paraphrases will tell us whether indeed they are understood as units of meaning. There is one more indicator for a true collocation: its availability for metaphorization processes. The second example demonstrates that friendly fire in German can now be used to refer to internecine warfare. As a metaphor, *friendly fire* loses the feature of 'accidental fire'; instead it refers to consciously hostile actions within a group. Here is another example, taken from Google:

> *Nicht alle 'Liberalen' sind eingeschwenkt. Aber das friendly fire schmerzt besonders. Merkels Kandidatur ist streitbesetzt.* ('Not all "liberals" [within the Christian Democratic Party] could be won over. But the friendly fire is particularly painful. [Party chair] Merkel's candidature is controversial.')

The same metaphorical usage is also found in English texts. Here is an example taken from Google:

> Defence Secretary Geoff Hoon faced questions about the deployment, why it happened so quickly, what his exit strategy was and how long it would last – all of which he had answered in previous exchanges.
> But his opposite number, Bernard Jenkin, offered his overall support for the operation.
> There was not even much friendly fire from Mr Hoon's own benches.

In this section we have explored *friendly fire* in a monolingual and a bilingual context with the aim of finding criteria that set apart statistically significant, but contingent, co-occurrences of two or more words from semantically relevant collocations, also called fixed expressions. There are two approaches. If we look at meaning from the perspective of usage, we find that there are good reasons of simplicity to assign collocation status to those expressions which, taken as a whole, are monosemous. The phrase *friendly fire* belongs here; a collocation analysis will reveal that it (almost) always occurs in comparable contexts. This perspective is decisive for the computational processing of natural language; as we will see, it facilitates computer-aided translation.

From the perspective of language understanding, the prime criterion for assigning collocation status to lexical co-occurrence patterns is paraphrase. If we find that a phrase is repeatedly paraphrased as a unit of meaning, we have a reason to assume that it is a single lexical item. A supporting criterion is that the phrase, as a whole, can be used in a metaphorical way. This is, as we have seen, the case for both *false dawn* and *friendly fire*. A third criterion is specific to a bilingual perspective. It seems that the translation equivalent of a true collocation is not what would be the most appropriate translation if each of the elements were translated separately. If it were, we would expect, as the equivalent of *friendly fire*, the German phrase *befreundetes Feuer*, for which we found only one occurrence. Rather, collocations are translated as a whole, and it does not seem to matter whether the favoured equivalent makes any sense if interpreted literally as a combination of the elements involved. The phrase *freundliches Feuer* is, if taken literally, seriously misleading. For a new unit of meaning, this does not matter; the unit will mean whatever is acceptable to the discourse community. Finally, the high frequency of the English phrase *friendly fire* in German texts suggests that there is no acceptable autochthonous German equivalent and that the English phrase therefore has to be imported.

Is *friendly fire* a true collocation? 'True' collocations can be shown to be not only statistically significant but also semantically relevant. Semantic relevance can be demonstrated both for the methodological approach and for the theoretical approach to the definition of units of meaning. The analysis presented here has demonstrated that the concept of the unit of meaning as the criterion for fixed expressions is not arbitrary. Corpus linguistics can make an enormous impact on lexicography. It can change our understanding of the vocabulary of a natural language. We can overcome the unfortunate situation that most of the (more common) lexical items in the dictionaries are polysemous. The ambiguity we had to deal with in traditional linguistics will disappear once we replace the medieval concept of the single word by the new concept of a collocation or a unit of meaning. Instead of choosing among four senses for *friendly* and eight senses for *fire*, we end up with one single meaning for the fixed expression *friendly fire*.

2.7 Collocations, translation and parallel corpora

In this section, we will address the methodological aspect of working with collocations. Our aim is to demonstrate the impact which the appreciation of the collocation phenomenon can have on translation. As empirical bases, we will produce evidence from several parallel corpora. To work with these corpora, we have to align each text and its translation first on a sentence-to-sentence level and then on the level of the lexical item, be it a single word, or an idiom, or a 'true' collocation – in short, on the level of the unit of meaning.

All those who have ever translated a text into their own or a foreign language know that we do not translate word by word. Nevertheless, our traditional translation aid is the bilingual dictionary. Most entries, by far, are single words, and for most of the words we find many alternatives for how to translate them. In most cases, the dictionary cannot tell us which of the alternatives we have to choose in a particular case. This is why bilingual dictionaries are not very helpful when the target language is not our native language. We do not translate single words in isolation but units that are large enough to be monosemous, so that for them there is only one translation equivalent in the target language, or, if there are more, then these equivalents will be reckoned as synonymous.

We call these units translation units. Are they the same as units of meaning? Not quite. Natural languages cannot be simply mapped onto each other. The ongoing negotiations among the members of a discourse community lead to results which cannot be predicted. Languages go different ways. They construe different realities. According to most monolingual English dictionaries, the word *bone* seems to be a unit of meaning, described in the *NODE* as 'any of the pieces of hard, whitish tissue making up the skeleton in humans and other vertebrates'. This accurately describes the way *bone* is used in English. From a German perspective, however, *bone* has, traditionally speaking, three different meanings; there are three non-synonymous translation equivalents for it. In the context of fish (or any of its hyponyms), Germans use the word *Gräte*. In the context of non-fishy animals, dead or alive, and of live humans, they call a bone *Knochen*. In the context of the bones of the deceased, the German word is *Gebeine*. For translating into German, the relevant unit of meaning therefore is *bone* plus all the context words that help to make the proper choice among the three German equivalents. What we come up with in our source text is (probably) not a fixed expression, a collocation of the type *false dawn* or *friendly fire*, but rather a set of words (collocates) we find in the close vicinity of *bone*. Thus in Google we find:

> The poor were initially buried in areas in the churchyard or near the church. From time to time, the bones (*Gebeine*) were dug up and then laid out

in a tasteful and decorative manner in the charnel house.

Then place trout on a plate and run a knife along each side of ... Sever head, fins and remove skin with a fork. All you have left is great eating with no bones (*Gräten*).

We expect a person to say she feels terrible after breaking a bone (*Knochen*).

The word in italics indicates the appropriate German translation in each case. A suitable parallel corpus would give us a sufficient number of occurrences for each of the three translation equivalents. Once we have found all the instances of *Gräte(n)* we can then search for *bone(s)* in the aligned English sentence and set up the collocation profile of *bone* when translated as *Gräte*. Such a collocation profile is a list of all words found in the immediate context of the keyword (*bone* in our case), listed according to their statistical significance as collocates of the keyword. The collocation profile of bone as the equivalent of *Gräte* will contain words like *trout, salmon, eat, fin, remove*, etc. A dictionary of translation units would give, for each keyword which is ambiguous relative to the target language, the collocation profile going with each of the equivalents. The users then have to check which of the words contained in the collocation profiles occur in the context of the word they are about to translate, and the choice can then be made almost mechanically. These combinations of a keyword together with their (statistically significant) collocates are also called collocations. Thus we find two kinds of collocations: those which can be described as fixed expressions and to which a grammatical pattern can be assigned (*false dawn*: adjective + noun) and those of which we can say only that the collocates are found in the immediate context of the keyword (e.g. *trout* in the context of *bone*).

Both kinds of collocations have in common that they are monosemous, either in a monolingual or in a bilingual perspective, and that they therefore represent units of meaning or translation units.

The parallel corpora we are working with have been compiled from selections of the legal documents issued by the European Commission and excerpts from the proceedings of the European Parliament, together with some reports issued by them. They do not talk much about bones. This is why we chose another keyword, French *travail/travaux*. We have included the plural *travaux* in our analysis, because the plural is often rendered as a singular when translated into English. The default translation is *Arbeit* in German, while for English there are two main translation equivalents: *work* and *labour*. When do we translate *travail/travaux* as *work*, when as *labour*? The parallel corpus allows us to set up the relevant collocation profiles, on the basis of an analysis of a context span of five words to the left and five words to the right of the keyword:

Travail/travaux translated as *work*	*Travail/travaux* translated as *labour*
Programme (410)	Marché (747)
Commission (255)	Ministre (170)
Conseil (212)	Marchés (151)
Cours (123)	Sociales (125)
Organisation (122)	Affaires (117)
Préparatoires (113)	Emploi (88)
Vue (109)	Forces (65)
Groupe (108)	Normes (60)
Temps (99)	Femmes (60)
Sécurité (97)	Sociale (50)

For each of the collocation profiles, we have selected the ten most frequent words (other than grammatical words

117

like articles and prepositions) found in the context. The frequency of each item is given in brackets. The most amazing finding is that there is no overlap at all between the two profiles. This is striking evidence that *travail/ travaux* occurs in different contexts when it is translated as *work* from those when it is translated as *labour*. Do the collocation profiles help with translation? Here are two French sentences, one in which *travaux* corresponds to *work*, one in which *travail* corresponds to *labour*:

> *WORK: La réforme du fonctionnement du Conseil soit opérée indépendamment des travaux préparatoires en vue de la future conférence intergouvernementale.*

> *LABOUR: Le Comité permanent de l'emploi s'est réuni aujourdhui sous la présidence de M. Walter Riester, ministre fédéral du travail et des affaires sociales d'Allemagne.*

Indeed, the collocation-profile approach to translation seems to work. This has little to do with our human understanding of meaning. In the first example, we find *vue*, part of the fixed expression *en vue de,* a prepositional expression meaning 'in the face of'. This is in no way semantically connected with *travaux* meaning 'work'. That it is part of the profile is contingent to our corpus. Also, there seems no sound reason why *travaux* in the context of *Conseil* should be translated as *work* and not as *labour*. It just happens to be that way.

Again, in the second example there is no obvious reason why *emploi* would necessitate the equivalent *labour*. It just so happens that in 88 cases where we find *emploi* close to *travail/travaux*, we find *labour* and not *work* in the translation. The real reason is a different one: *le ministre du travail* is a named entity in the form of a fixed expression for which the equivalent in English is 'Minister of Labour' or 'Secretary of Labour'. What we learn here is that the methodological approach to collocation analysis, the approach based on usage rather than on paraphrase, is a technical operation whose results do not map well onto human understanding.

Investigations of translation equivalence based on parallel corpora are still very much in their infancy. The collocation profiles have to become more refined. The goal is to increase their significance by allocating positions in grammatical patterns to the lexical elements they contain. For the time being our parallel corpora are too small for that. Once they can compare in size with our monolingual corpora we may well find out that the kind of collocations which are not fixed expressions (like *travail*/*travaux* and its collocates as they appear in a collocation profile) can be better described as 'true collocations' conforming to a specific grammatical pattern. Thus, in the first sentence, we find *travaux préparatoires*. This phrase can be seen as a monosemous fixed expression, a unit of meaning, conforming to the adjective + noun pattern, and indeed it is (almost) always rendered as *preparatory work* in our parallel corpus.

Parallel corpora monitor the practice of translation. Because they often cannot rely on bilingual dictionaries, translators have to acquire a competence that is the result of experience and interaction with other members of the bilingual discourse community of which they are a part. In their work, they aim to reflect the conventions upon which this community has agreed. The methodology of corpus linguistics enables us to tap this expertise. Our goal is, as we have said above, to replace the single-word entries of current bilingual dictionaries with entries of translation units. The results can be impressive. In a final example, we will use a small French–German parallel corpus. The word we have chosen is *exclusion*, meaning roughly the same as its English counterpart. For the single word we will find an astonishing variety of equivalents. But this diversity disappears once we replace the single word by a collocation of which it is a part. In our example, the fixed expression is *exclusion sociale*. For it, we find only one German equivalent: *soziale Ausgrenzung*. From our bilingual perspective, this proves that *exclusion sociale* is, indeed, a 'true' collocation. It is monosemous; it is a unit of meaning.

To begin, here are some corpus extracts, in the form of a KWIC (key word in context)–concordance, demonstrating the diversity:

extraites pour la vente, à l'exclusion des activités de transformation
den Verkauf mit Ausnahme der Tätigkeiten zur Weiterverarbeitung
['with the exception of activities']

qui résulte de leur travail, à l'exclusion de l'irradiation résultant
wobei Bestrahlung durch Grundstrahlung unberücksichtigt bleiben
['remain ignored']

roïde, la peau ou le tissu osseux, à l'exclusion des extrémités désignées
so Bestrahlung anderer Organe oder Gewebe als Extremitäten
['other organs or tissues than']

des concertations qui débouchent sur l'exclusion de ceux qui sont
deren Ergebnis die Arbeitslosen ausgeschlossen werden
['are being excluded']

il nous manque le combat contre l'exclusion des travailleurs plus âgés
uns fehlt die Bekämpfung der Ausgrenzung von älteren Beschäftigten
['exclusion']

de viandes de gibier sauvage à l'exclusion des
viandes de porcin sauvage
von Wildfleisch, ausgenommen Wildschweinfleisch,
aus Drittländern
['except boar meat']

This is only a small selection of the variety encountered; all citations are taken from the first ten instances. All translations are perfectly viable. Within their contexts, they are certainly appropriate. Only one of them, we should add, features in the largest French–German dictionary, the *Sachs–Villatte* (1st edition 1979): *mit Ausnahme von/der* as the equivalent of the phrase *à l'exclusion de*. In our few lines, we have four occurrences of this French phrase; and each time it is translated differently. We also find *Ausschluss, Ausschließung, Verweisung*, but no *Ausgrenzung*. Traditional bilingual dictionaries also tend to overlook the fact that it often makes sense to translate a noun phrase (*sur l'exclusion de ceux*) by a verb phrase (*ausgeschlossen werden* ['are being excluded']).

Once we move on to the collocation *exclusion sociale*, the result is straightforward. In 29 of the total of 31 occurrences in our small corpus, we find *soziale Ausgrenzung* as the German equivalent. In the remaining two instances, the adjective has been turned into an adverb modifying the verb. This is a representative selection of our findings:

```
   diese Opfer sozialer Ausgrenzung für immer ausgeschlos
und der Gefahr sozialer Ausgrenzung entgegengewirkt wird.
 Kampf gegen die soziale Ausgrenzung in ihren verschiedenen
das Problem der sozialen Ausgrenzung junger Leute
Vermeidung der sozialen Ausgrenzung, sind in einer
   von Armut und sozialer Ausgrenzung ist.
Bekämpfung der sozialen Ausgrenzung.
Armut und der sozialen Ausgrenzung. In der EU leben
```

2.8 Conclusion: from meaning to understanding

From a corpus linguistics perspective, the meaning of a unit of meaning is what we can glean from the discourse. It is what we can find out about how a unit of meaning is being used. More important than the plain usage data are the paraphrases of a unit of meaning. They explain to us what this unit means; they attempt to define it; they tell us how this unit is semantically related to other units of meaning. A whole book can be a paraphrase. All those books about globalization try to explain to their audiences what *globalization* means. Indeed, the conflation of linguistic knowledge with encyclopaedic knowledge is one of the major axioms of corpus linguistics.

It is impossible to compile the complete meaning of a unit of meaning. We cannot have access to more than a tiny fraction of the discourse. Therefore we will never capture all the paraphrases that the discourse contains for a given unit of meaning. Corpora, be they as large as we might imagine, will only ever provide a glimpse of what has been said. This shouldn't deter us. The relevance principle of corpus linguistics assures us that whatever is thought to be important will be repeated in other texts. Once our corpus is large enough to display a certain saturation of paraphrases, we can rest assured that what is missing is at least not the mainstream understanding of our unit of meaning.

It is unlikely that any two persons have been exposed to exactly the same discourse events. Once they discuss the meaning of a unit of meaning, their views are bound to differ. They may have heard some identical paraphrases or some that are similar, but each of them will also have heard paraphrases that the other person hasn't. Each of them will subscribe to some paraphrases and will object to others. This is why it is highly unlikely that two people will ever entirely agree on what a unit of meaning means. There is no one description that will completely cover what the unit means. The discourse community is a community of autonomous members. So if two persons want to achieve an agreement on what a unit of meaning such as *globalization* means, they have to negotiate. The result of their negotiation won't necessarily be that there is only one way to paraphrase *globalization*; they could also agree that there are two or three competing paraphrases, partially overlapping, partially contradicting each other.

Wouldn't that mean that such a unit of meaning has not one, but two, or three, or many meanings? Wouldn't that contradict our claim that units of meaning have only one meaning, and that, therefore, linguists shouldn't be concerned about lexical ambiguity? Whether a chunk, a conglomerate of words (or, for that matter, a single word) is a unit of meaning is not a matter of identical paraphrases, it is a matter of usage. There might be a dozen different paraphrases for *globalization*; as long as all occurrences of *globalization* display the same usage pattern, it will continue to be counted as one unit of meaning. Only if two (or more) usage patterns emerge is there ambiguity. Then we are forced to add more lexical elements to the chunk or conglomerate, until again for this larger unit we find only one usage pattern.

Even if there are no two people for whom a unit of meaning means exactly the same, meaning is still a social and not a mental phenomenon. All the paraphrases of a unit of meaning are part of the same discourse. But no member of the discourse community will have been exposed to all of them. If we ask any member of the discourse community what *globalization* means, they might provide us with yet another paraphrase, and this paraphrase would, of course, also become part of the discourse and thus be available to other members of the discourse community. They would probably attempt to describe as closely as they could how they understood *globalization*. But a paraphrase can never be more than one voice among many.

Paraphrases are exclusively verbal. They are part of the discourse. My understanding of a unit of meaning, however, is private. It normally involves a lot of what is not verbal and what cannot be easily verbalized. Your understanding of *globalization* will originate from the paraphrases you have heard, but it will not stop there. As all these paraphrases tell you something different, you're forced to make up your own mind. While trying to make sense of these paraphrases, you'll use your own judgement. When some people paraphrase *globalization*, you may have more or less strong reservations. When they tell you that globalization leads to prosperity, you may associate that with an image of the poor in some underdeveloped country. Or you might think of multinational companies and of how they ruined the indigenous economy of the countries they did business with. However, you'll never be able to verbalize all the associations, all these flashes of memory that come to you whenever someone uses the word *globalization* in your company. How one understands a unit of meaning will always remain a first-person experience, accessible only to that person, in the same way as emotions are. Only I can really know how I feel grief, no matter how hard I try to explain what I feel to others. Only I can know how I experience globalization, when I am confronted with the word. People aren't machines. Even if they are fed with the same input they can come up with different conclusions.

The interesting question, then, is how do people develop their understanding of units of meaning? There was a time when we hadn't heard of the word *globalization*. Today, when we hear it, we think we understand it, and our understanding of it encompasses a lot more than what any dictionary definition would contain. Where do these associations come from? How did we arrive at this complex, fuzzy network of associations and images?

We would like to investigate this quandary by probing into the word *truth*. What does it mean, and how does its meaning relate to our understanding of this word? We will start with the definition we find in the *NODE* (here, and in subsequent quotes, leaving out technical details, examples and further senses):

> the quality or state of being true; that which is true or in accordance with fact or with reality; a fact or belief that is accepted as true

What does *true* mean?

> in accordance with fact or reality; real or actual

How are *fact* and *reality* defined?

> *fact*: a thing that is indisputably the case; the truth about events as opposed to the interpretation
> *reality*: the world or state of things as they actually exist, as opposed to an idealistic or notional state of them

What does *be the case* mean?

> be so

Finally, what is the meaning of *actual(ly)*?

> existing in fact, typically as contrasted with what was intended, expected or believed

The definitions are, as we can see, to a large extent circular. This, in itself, is not surprising. All dictionary definitions have to be circular; they are using the words which also have to be defined in the dictionary. What is surprising is the close circuit. *Truth* is defined by *true* and

125

by *fact* and *reality*; *true* is defined by *fact* and *reality*, and by *actual*; *fact* is defined by *be the case* (i.e. 'be so'), and by *truth*; *reality* is defined by *actual(ly)*; and *actual(ly)* is defined by *fact*. So *truth* is defined by *fact*, and *fact*, in turn, is defined by *truth*. Lexicographers normally try to avoid definitions with such close circles because they do not really help the user to understand the lexical item in question. However, in the case of words like *truth*, *fact* and *reality*, there seems to be no other way to proceed.

This set of definitions is not (and is not intended to be) equivalent to my (or anyone else's) understanding of the concept 'truth'. Truth, we no doubt all feel, is something immensely important and goes far beyond just being the case. Truth is a moral value, it is something people owe to each other, it is something very deep which needs to be explored responsibly, and it is not something we come across or appeal to when we deal with the mundane facts of everyday life like asking for a pint of ale.

Fortunately, the *NODE* gives us some hints that truth is not quite as simple as we have made it look in our summary of the dictionary definitions. This gives credit to the exceptional quality of this dictionary. *Truth*, we are told, can also mean a 'belief that is accepted as true', *truth* stands in opposition to *interpretation*, and it refers to reality as opposed to 'idealistic or notional' things, while *actual(ly)* refers to facts as opposed to 'what was intended, expected or believed'. So truth is opposed to what is just 'notional' or 'believed', or a subjective 'interpretation', and it can also be a 'belief' that is accepted (by whom?) as the truth. So *truth* is more than 'what is the case'. People can have conflicting ideas about what is true. There is a tension that seems to go along with this word; and the dictionary makes us aware that truth is a contentious issue. This is shared by my understanding of *truth*.

126

A look at the American *Random House College Dictionary* of 1975 (two-thirds of the size of *NODE*) shows definitions for the words in question that are, on the surface, very similar to the *NODE*. This is what we find for *truth* (here again, and in subsequent quotes, we leave out technical details, examples and further senses):

> 1. true or actual state of the matter. 2. conformity with fact or reality; verity. 3. a verified or indisputable fact, proposition, principle. 4. state or character of being true.

These are the definitions for *fact* and *reality*:

> *fact*: 1. the quality of existing or being real. 2. something known to exist or have happened. 3. a truth known by actual experience or by observation. 4. something said to be true or to have happened.
> *reality*: 1. the state or quality of being real. 2. resemblance to what is real. 3. a real thing or a fact.

It seems we also have to take into consideration the adjective *real*:

> 1. true, not merely ostensible or nominal. 2. actual rather than imaginary, ideal or fictitious. 3. having actual, rather than imaginary, existence. 5. genuine, authentic.

The other two words asking for definitions are *verity* and *verify*:

> *verity*: 1. the state or quality of being true. 2. something that is true, as a principle, a belief, or statement.
> *verify*: 1. to prove the truth of, confirm. 2. to ascertain the truth, or correctness of. 3. to act as ultimate proof or evidence of; serve to confirm.

127

On the whole, the Random House definitions seem to profess a stronger realism than the *NODE* ones. The 'true or actual state of a matter' is much more straightforward than 'the quality or state of being true; that which is true or in accordance with fact or with reality; a fact or belief that is accepted as true'. Something is true, or it is not. We are not made aware of the tension connected with *truth*. Where it comes in is in the first definition of *real*: 'true, not merely ... nominal'. But this allusion to the medieval battleground of realism versus nominalism presupposes an acquaintance with philosophy few people can claim; on others it is mostly lost. The discourse is brought in by the phrase *indisputable fact*, reminding us of the *NODE* phrase of something being 'indisputably the case'. It comes in much stronger in the definition 'something said to be true or to have happened'. But should we subscribe to this definition? Would we really say that a UFO incident was true because it is said by some people to have happened? The Random House definitions do not let us feel the tension that the *NODE* conveys – for instance, with its definition for *actual*: 'existing in fact, typically as contrasted with what was intended, expected or believed'.

When we ask ourselves how we understand the word *truth*, or what *truth* means to us personally, the mundane dictionary definitions with their close circular definitions will be about the last thing that comes to our mind. Truth, we feel, is something very important, something that is frequently at stake. It is a moral value. The way we will have first learned about truth may easily have been in the context of lying. Our parents, rightly interested in our whereabouts, wanted to make sure we would tell them the truth, and this is why they taught us lying is wrong. It is strange that neither of the dictionaries mentions *lies* in their definitions of truth. It certainly plays a very prominent role in my understanding of *truth*. In the Catechism of the Catholic Church we read:

> (2483) Lying is the most direct offence against truth. To lie is to speak or act against the truth in order to lead into error someone who has the right to know the truth.

This is a somewhat jesuitical way of putting it, in spite of being the received wisdom. Parents, we are told, do have the right to know the truth; children don't. Again tension comes in. Truth is never simple.

Understanding is a first-person experience. We will never be able to convey fully, verbally or in any other way, to other people how we understand a unit of meaning, just as we are not able to let anyone else know exactly what kind and intensity of pain we suffer. Our understanding of any unit of meaning is not something static that could be put into words. When we hear a unit of meaning, or a text sequence, or when we want to use a unit of meaning within a textual sequence, there are memories that come up, memories of events to which we were a witness or in which we played a part. Often what we think are genuine memories of an event itself are recollections of subsequent verbalizations of the event. All these memories involve images or other sensations, and while some of them refer to actual sensual data, others are largely imaginary. Another part of these memories will be memories of other people's contributions to the discourse, things we heard people say themselves, or things that were reported. These texts again, as we remember them, will evoke memories. It is our memory that forms our understanding. But we have little control over what we remember. Remembering is a combination of intention and randomness. It is not the result of an algorithmic procedure. Our understanding of a unit of meaning is nothing fixed. It depends on the situation, on how we feel, on what we want to do, and on innumerable other factors. Any new input will change our understanding. We never can understand a text when we read it a second time in the same way as we understood it as we read it the first time.

We would not know about truth without other people telling us what it is. It is the paraphrases, the explanations, the instructions we received from them that we remember and that evoke the memories of events we associate with them. These paraphrases are what constitute for us the meaning of a unit of meaning. As we have said often before, we have all been exposed to different sets of such paraphrases, and therefore a word such as *truth* may mean different things to different people. But what is worth remembering is also worth repeating. Therefore many of the paraphrases will strike a familiar chord even if we have never read the texts in which they occur.

To find paraphrases of the unit of meaning *truth*, we searched the Bank of English (BoE), with its 420 million words, for sentences beginning with '*Truth is*'. This is a very common pattern for opening up a paraphrase. All together, we found 159 occurrences of this phrase. Compared to the total number of occurrences of the word *truth* in the BoE, 34,645, this is only a tiny fraction. As it turned out, about half of the citations were not paraphrases at all. They were sentences like: *Truth is most of us have mediocre souls*. However, the remaining paraphrases still represent something of a common denominator of what truth means to all of us. At first glance it seems amazing that so few of them refer to what the dictionaries tell us. Perhaps it's not so strange, though. The definitions we find in the dictionaries are normally not controversial. So there is no point discussing them in the discourse community. Here, now, is a selection of paraphrases for truth, ordered loosely into seven pigeonholes. We've left out from these corpus citations what we deemed to be accidental and irrelevant.

(1) Truth is an emotional phenomenon
Truth is a force which pierces your heart, Vysotsky said.
Truth is mostly subjective and that's good when you are talking about music.
Truth is an attribute of love. Love is not complete without truth. The truth never hurts another person.

(2) Truth is a spiritual phenomenon
Truth is a totem to Murphy: artistic and spiritual truth, rather than mere accuracy.
Truth is always before us: the truth of God is bigger and smaller than all our formulations, however precious they may be.
Truth is one of the first casualties of secularism.
Truth is our king, the rest is nothing.
'Truth is our king.' Truth was holy, and cloud-cuckoo-land was silly, and blasphemy too.

(3) Truth is ugly
Truth is full of warts, and worse. It is a heap of dirt, sucked dry by Ariadne's kiss.
Truth is horrible. We live in an empty and meaningless cosmos where we can only expect to suffer.
Truth is not Beauty. It is something to be hidden in the deepest depths of one's inmost being.

(4) Truth is elusive
Truth is a black cat in a darkened room and justice is a blind bat, said Bertolt Brecht.
Great Britain spent centuries making modifications to the ancient system of trial by combat.
Truth is immaterial and, often, so is justice.
Truth is the most fragile of ideas.

(5) Truth is relative
Truth is always relative.
Truth is an immensely personal matter – what is true for me is not necessarily true for you.
Truth is, in fact, a product of dispute.
Truth is sought in a joint quest and effort.
Truth is a victim of time.
Truth is something complicated, something to be sought out.
Truth is provisional, Mr Rushdie seems to be saying.
(6) Truth is absolute
Truth is absolute.
Truth is blindingly obvious once you've recognised it.
Truth is established rationally, by proof.
Truth is normatively consonant with warranted assertability.
Truth is truth, in Malaysia or in Manchester.
(7) Truth is a many splendoured thing
Truth is a difficult concept.
Truth is a problem.
Truth is at stake.
Truth is the main thing. Lenin said: More light! Let the party know everything!
Truth is the foundation of trust.
Truth is manly.
Truth is often stranger than fiction.
Truth is what the masses like.
Truth is not a priority.

All these statements are part of the meaning of truth. We could not have heard them all. But all are part of the discourse. Many of them will sound familiar. Google has ca 1,340,000 hits for *truth* + '*stranger than fiction*'. Similar figures would be found for many other paraphrases. Even the phrase 'Truth is normatively consonant with warranted assertability' is not as singular as it looks; Google has 36 hits for '*truth consonant warranted assertability*'. What has caught the attention of people will be endlessly repeated in the discourse. It will leave traces in many texts.

As we see it, understanding a unit of meaning is a feature of our memories. Part of it is verbal input, what we have gleaned from the discourse. This is the part that constitutes what the unit means for each of us individually. It is what we can convey verbally, by repeating it verbatim or by rephrasing it. The other part of understanding is constituted by the memories that are evoked by hearing or saying a unit of meaning in a given situation. These memories are fuzzy and unstable, they are full of holes and constantly shifting. They are true first-person experiences. Try as we can, we will never be able to relate them faithfully to others. This doesn't mean they cannot be verbalized. We will refer to them whenever we discuss truth with other members of the discourse community. These textual sequences will enrich the discourse on truth, and they may well change what *truth* means, for those who hear them and for ourselves. The third part of our understanding of a unit of meaning is our rationalization of the verbal input and of the memories it evokes. We don't have to accept everything we're being told. We can form our own opinion, and that can differ more or less from the mainstream meaning of that unit. We can contribute our own paraphrase of *truth*. If it differs a lot from what others believe, they will probably reject it. Then it won't leave traces in subsequent texts. But our understanding of paraphrase may just differ modestly from what *truth* means to other people. If it catches their attention, if it expresses an idea that lies in the air, if it reverberates the Zeitgeist, then it may be picked up by others, and it may even change the mainstream meaning.

133

For corpus linguistics, meaning is a social phenomenon. It is the members of the language community
who negotiate what units of meaning mean. What a unit
of meaning means is the result of a democratic process.
Everyone has, or should have, a voice in it. Meaning is
not a matter for experts, self-appointed or otherwise. We
do not have to accept that the meaning of *murder*
includes abortion. There is no truth in the matter of
meaning, and there is no legitimate coercion to agree on a
definition. We do not have to accept that *property* is an
inviolate right. We can also say that all *property* is theft.
Both views are equally legitimate. What we have to learn
is what it takes to make our paraphrases palatable to the
other members of the discourse community. Education is
about learning to exercise one's rights as a free citizen in
a responsible way. Corpus linguistics puts us into a
position where we can inform ourselves what use others
have made of language. This knowledge empowers us to
contribute successfully to the discourse of which we are
members.

Further reading

The most prominent figure in corpus linguistics is, no doubt, John Sinclair. One of the most quoted works is probably his seminal book *Corpus Concordance Collocation* (1991). Sinclair's original and insightful thinking has influenced many linguists. A collection of his articles has recently been published in the book *Trust the Text. Language, Corpus and Discourse* (2004).

The best way to find out more about corpus linguistics is your own corpus research. This, however, may not be easy without proper guidance. An excellent book to learn how to work with language corpora is, for example, John Sinclair's *Reading Concordances* (2003), which provides many examples and is written in an easily accessible way.

The issue of representativeness is discussed by many authors and you may like to have a look, for instance, at Douglas Biber's article *Representativeness in corpus design* (1993). Other relevant works dealing with this topic are e.g. *Corpus Linguistics: Investigating Language Structure and Use* by Biber, Conrad and Reppen (1998), *An Introduction to Corpus Linguistics* by Kennedy (1998), the article by Geoffrey Leech *The state of art in corpus linguistics* (1991) and the chapter by Antoinette Renouf in *Looking Up* (1987).

If you are after more technical information on corpus mark-up, a clear, brief and not too technical overview is offered by the book *Corpus-Based Language Studies* by McEnery et al (2006). This book also discusses advantages and disadvantages of corpus annotation, such as POS tagging (adding information on parts-of-speech), lemmatization (grouping word forms under one lexeme), and parsing (syntactic analysis). Corpus annotation is not an uncontroversial issue and criticism mainly comes from linguists representing the corpus-driven approach (see below).

Today's corpora are often huge and one of the main problems for a corpus linguist is how to process such an amount of data. Thus, statistics plays an important role. Frequency of occurrence of recurrent language patterns is of central importance. However, as in any discipline where statistical methods are used, statistics can be enormously helpful but without proper interpretation and context can easily distort the overall picture. A very brief introduction to statistical methods used in corpus linguistics is provided by the above mentioned book *Corpus-Based Language Studies.* If you would like to go a step further, try Oakes' *Statistics for Corpus Linguistics* (1998).

Corpora are gradually becoming a part of most linguistic research. They are now being extensively used in applied linguistics as well. The area of language teaching and learning has developed its own learner corpora, translation studies makes use of parallel corpora, and corpora have become an essential tool in modern lexicography. To find out about corpus linguistics and language teaching, have a look at, for example, *How to Use Corpora in Language Teaching* (Sinclair (ed.), 2004) and *Computer Learner Corpora, Second Language Acquisition and Foreign Language Teaching* (Granger, Hung and Petch-Tyson (eds), 2002).

It is not doubted any more that corpora bring new possibilities to language studies. Corpora have opened up and revolutionized linguistics. But the field of corpus linguistics itself has changed enormously. It has been seen primarily as a set of methods and many linguists still do not acknowledge corpus linguistics as more than having a methodogical status (McEnery et al 2006: 8). Be it a theory or conceptual framework, corpus linguistics offers a perspective on language that sets it apart from received views or the views of cognitive linguistics, both relying heavily on introspection rather than natural language data (Teubert 2005: 2). Corpus linguistics thus stands against intuition- and introspection-based linguistic studies but within the field itself there are two main approaches: the corpus-based and corpus-driven. The latter, being the more radical, has been defined by Tognini-Bonelli (2001: 87) as aiming to derive linguistic categories systematically from the recurrent patterns and the frequency distributions that emerge from language in context.

Corpus linguistics sees language as a social phenomenon and its focus is on meaning. Meaning and form cannot be separated and, unlike traditional linguistics, the corpus linguistic description of language prioritizes lexis. However, the field of corpus linguistics is today very diverse and the amount of writing concerned with corpus linguistics is rapidly growing. Any selection of recommended books and articles will be always incomplete; the selection above gives a good starting point for the exploration of corpus linguistics.

Glossary

alignment
the process of aligning equivalent units in bilingual or multilingual **parallel corpora**, so that a unit in one language corresponds to the equivalent unit in another language and both of them can be accessed or displayed at the same time.

annotation
corpus-external information added to a **corpus**, such as **tagging** or information identifying the origin and nature of the text.

antonymy
the relationship of oppositeness in meaning, as in English between the words *good* and *bad* or *buy* and *sell*.

cognate, cognate word
(1) a word related to one or more other words in the same language by derivation, as in English *thought* is a cognate of *think*.
(2) a word which shares a common ancestor with one or more other words, as with English *sleep*, Dutch *slaap* and German *Schlaf*, which are all considered to be descended from an ancestral Germanic form.

cognitive linguistics
a branch of linguistics or cognitive science which seeks to explain language in terms of mental processes or with reference to a mental reality underlying language.

collocate
a word repeatedly found in the close vicinity of a node word in texts; for example, in English the words *partial, lunar, solar* are collocates of the word *eclipse*.

collocation
the habitual meaningful co-occurrence of two or more words (a

node word and its **collocate** or **collocates**) in close proximity to each other; as a lexical relationship, **collocation** can be defined quantitatively as the degree to which the probability of a word *y* occurring in text is increased by the presence of another word *x*.

collocation profile
a computer-generated list of all the **collocates** of a node word in a **corpus**, usually listed in the order of their statistical significance of occurrence.

concordance
a list of lines of text containing a node word, nowadays generated by computer as the principal output of a search of a **corpus** showing the word in its contexts and thus representing a sum of its usage; see also **KWIC**.

content word
a word with a relatively clear meaning of its own, in contrast to a **function word**.

corpus
a collection of naturally occurring language texts in electronic form, often compiled according to specific design criteria and typically containing many millions of words.

discourse
the totality of verbal interactions and activities (spoken and written) that have taken place and are taking place in a language community.

etymology
an account of the historical origin and development of a word.

fixed expression
a co-occurrence of two or more words which forms a unit of meaning.

function word
a word with a relatively general meaning serving to express functions such as grammatical relationships, as in English the words *for*, *to*, *the*, in contrast to a **content word**.

generative
(of a grammar or a finite set of formal rules) capable of generating an infinite set of grammatical sentences in a language.

hapax legomenon
a word or form found only once in a body of texts; for example; in a **corpus** or in the works of a single author.

hyponymy
the relationship of meaning between specific and general words; for example, in English *rose* is a hyponym of *flower*

idiom
a type of **fixed expression** in which the meaning cannot be deduced from the meanings or functions of the different parts of the expression, as with the English idiom *kick someone upstairs* meaning 'move someone to what seems to be a more important post but with the motive of removing them from their current post'.

KWIC (short for **key word in context**)
a computer-generated set of **concordance** lines in which the node word is in the centre of each line.

lemma
a form which represents different forms of a lexical entry in a dictionary, as with the English lemma *bring* representing *bring*, *brings*, *bringing* and *brought*.

lexical item
a word understood as a unit of meaning rather than as a written or spoken form.

lexicogrammar
the **lexicon** and grammar of a language, taken together as an integrated system.

lexicon
the vocabulary or word stock of a language, usually understood as a lexical system or as part of **lexicogrammar**.

lexicology
the study of the **lexicon**.

lexicography
the art and science of dictionary-making.

mentalism
the belief in the reality of the human mind and in the possibility and importance of systematically investigating its nature.

meronymy
the relationship of meaning between part and whole, as in English between the words *arm* and *body* or *sole* and *shoe*.

monitor corpus
a **corpus** which contains specimens of language taken from different times (and is ideally regularly updated) and which thus assists the study of language change.

morpheme
the smallest element of language which carries a meaning or function, including **affixes** such as *pre-* or *-ed* as well as irreducible words such as *want* or *white*.

neologism
a new word, form, construction or sense introduced into **discourse** and ultimately into the language.

opportunistic corpus
a **corpus** which makes use of existing and readily available resources, does not claim to be representative, and reflects the assumption that every corpus is inevitably imbalanced.

paradigm
a set of forms, usually grammatically conditioned, based on a single **lexical item**, as in English the set *chase, chasing, chased* or *want, wanting, wanted*.

parallel corpus
a **corpus** which contains equivalent and usually **aligned** texts in two or more languages; it is sometimes called a **translation corpus** but does not always include the original text as well as translations of it.

parsing
grammatical analysis of a text, usually with the principal aim
of identifying elements as subjects, nouns, verbs, and so on.

part of speech = word class

qualia
the felt qualities associated with experiences, such as the
feeling of a pain, or the hearing of a sound, which are
expressed by specific words.

reference corpus
a **corpus** which aims to be balanced and to reflect the contemporary language.

semantics
the systematic study of meaning in language.

special corpus
a **corpus** built for a special research purpose.

synonymy
the relationship of identity (or more realistically of near
identity) in meaning, as in English between *dentures* and *false
teeth* or *often* and *frequently*.

tagging
attaching grammatical labels, usually indicating **word classes**,
to words in a **corpus**, usually by automatic methods.

term
a word with a meaning that is relatively precise and independent of the context, often subject to some special convention or regulation, as, for example, with technical terms
defined by standards associations.

thesaurus
a reference work in which words are grouped by meaning
rather than listed alphabetically.

translation corpus
a **corpus** which contains an original text and at least one
translation of it into another language; see also **parallel corpus**.

word class
a small set of grammatical categories to which words can be allocated, varying from language to language but usually including such classes as noun, verb and adjective; also known as **part of speech**.

References

Aarts, J., P. de Haan and N. Oostdijk (eds), 1992, *English Language Corpora: Design, Analysis and Exploitation*, Papers from the Thirteenth International Conference on English Language Research on Computerized Corpora, Rodopi, Amsterdam.

Biber, Doug, 1993, 'Representativeness in corpus design', *Literary and Linguistic Computing* 8(4), 243–57.

Biber, D., S. Conrad and R. Reppen, 1998, *Corpus Linguistics: Investigating Language Structure and Use*, Cambridge University Press, Cambridge.

Biber, Douglas, Stig Johansson, Geoffrey Leech, Susan Conrad and Edward Finegan, 1999, *Longman Grammar of Spoken and Written English*, Pearson Education, Harlow, England.

Calzolari, N., M. Baker and T. Kruyt (eds), 1995, *Towards a Network of European Reference Corpora*, Linguistica Computazionale Vol. XI–XII, Giardini Editori e Stampatori, Pisa.

Carroll, Lewis, 1994, *Alice Through the Looking Glass*, Penguin Popular Classics, London.

Catechism of the Catholic Church, 1995, available online (www.christusrex.org).

Chomsky, Noam, 1957, *Syntactic Structures*, HarperCollins Publishers, New York and Glasgow.

Chomsky, Noam, 1965, *Aspects of the Theory of Syntax*, MIT Press, Cambridge, Massachusetts.

Chomsky, Noam, 2000, *New Horizons in the Study of Language and Mind*, Cambridge University Press, Cambridge, Massachusetts.

Collins COBUILD English Language Dictionary, 1987, editor-in-chief John Sinclair, HarperCollins, London.

Collins Dictionary of the English Language, 1979, edited by Patrick Hanks, William Collins, Glasgow.

Collins–Robert French Dictionary, 1998 (5th edn), HarperCollins, London.

Culler, Jonathan, 1976, *Saussure*, Fontana Modern Masters, William Collins, Glasgow.

Dennett, D. C., 1993, *Consciousness Explained*, Penguin, London.

Edmonds, P., 2002, Introduction to SENSEVAL, *ELRA Newsletter*, October 2002.

Fellbaum, C. (ed.), 1998, *WordNet: an Electronic Lexical Database*, MIT Press, Cambridge, Massachusetts.

Firth, J. R., 1957, *Papers in Linguistics 1934–1951*, Longman, London.

Fodor, J. A., 1975, *The Language of Thought*, MIT Press, Cambridge, Massachusetts.

Fodor, J. A., 1994, *The Elm and the Expert: Mentalese and its Semantics*, MIT Press, Cambridge, Massachusetts.

Fodor, J. A., 1998, *Concepts; Where Cognitive Science Went Wrong*, 1996 John Locke Lectures, Oxford University Press, Oxford.

Fodor, J. A. and E. Lepore, 2002, *The Compositionality Papers*, Oxford University Press, Oxford.

Fries, Charles C., 1940, *American English Grammar*, Appleton Century Crofts, New York.

Fries, U., G. Tottie and P. Schneider (eds), 1993, *Creating and Using English Language Corpora*, Papers from the Fourteenth International Conference on English Language Research on Computerized Corpora, Zürich, Rodopi, Amsterdam.

Goody, J., 2000, *The Power of Written Tradition*, Smithsonian Institute Press, Washington and London.

Granger, S., J. Hung and S. Petch-Tyson (eds), 2002, *Computer Leaner Corpora, Second Language Acquisition and Foreign Language Teaching*, John Benjamins, Philadelphia.

Hunston, Susan and Gill Francis, 2000, *Pattern Grammar: a Corpus-Driven Approach to the Lexical Grammar of English*, John Benjamins, Amsterdam and Philadelphia.

Johansson, S., G. Leech and H. Goodluck, 1978, *Manual of Information to Accompany the Lancaster–Oslo/Bergen Corpus of British English, for Use With Digital Computers*, University of Oslo, Department of English, Oslo, available online (http://khnt.hit.uib.no/icame/manuals/lob/INDEX.HTM).

Johnson's Dictionary: A Modern Selection by E. L. McAdam and George Milne, 1995, Cassell, London.

Keller, R., 1998, *A Theory of Linguistic Signs*, Oxford University Press, Oxford.

Kennedy, G., 1998, *An Introduction to Corpus Linguistics*, Longman, London and New York.

Krishnamurthy, R. (ed.), 2004, *English Collocation Studies: the OSTI Report* (new edition of Sinclair, J., S. Jones and R. Daley, 1970, English Lexical Studies: Report to OSTI on Project C/LP/08). London and New York: Continuum.

Lakoff, G., 1987, *Women, Fire, and Dangerous Things*, University of Chicago Press, Chicago.

Langenscheidts Großwörterbuch Französisch (Sachs–Vilatte), 1979, Teil 1: Französisch–Deutsch, Völlige Neubearbeitung, Teil 2: Deutsch–Französisch, Völlige Neubearbeitung 1968 mit Nachtrag 1979, Langenscheidt, Berlin and Munich.

Leech, G., 'The state of art in corpus linguistics', in K. Aijmer and B. Altenberg (eds), *English Corpus Linguistics. Studies in Honour of Jan Svartvik*, Longman, London, pp.8–29.

Levitt, T., 1983, The Globalization of Markets, *Harvard Business Review* 6 (3), May–June 1983.

Lewis, Charlton T. and Charles Short, 1879, *A Latin Dictionary: Founded on Andrews' Edition of Freund's Latin Dictionary, Revised, Enlarged and in great part Rewritten by Charlton T. Lewis and Charles Short*, Oxford University Press, Oxford. (Various editions published later.)

Liddell, Henry George and Robert Scott, 1843, *Greek–English Lexicon*, Oxford University Press, Oxford. (Various editions published later.)

Littré, Emile, 1863–73, *Dictionnaire de la Langue Française* (Supplement published 1878 and various editions published later.)

Longman Dictionary of Contemporary English, 1987 (new edn), editorial director Della Summers, Longman, Harlow.

Longman Dictionary of English Idioms, 1979, Longman, Harlow and London.

McEnery, T. and A. Wilson, 1996, *Corpus Linguistics*, Edinburgh University Press, Edinburgh.

McEnery, T., R. Xiao and Y. Tono, 2006, *Corpus-Based Language Studies*, Routledge, London and New York.

Macmillan English Dictionary for Advanced Learners, 2002, Macmillan Publishers, Oxford.

Macquarie Dictionary, 1997 (3rd edn), editor in chief Arthur Delbridge, Macquarie Library, Sydney.

Mayr, E., 2002, *What Evolution Is*, Weidenfeld & Nicholson, London.

Millar, S., 2003, The Language of War, *Guardian*, 24 March 2003.

Miller, K. L., 2002, The New Buzzword: Globaloney, *Newsweek*, Special Edition, December 2002–February 2003.

Moon, R., 1998, *Fixed Expressions and Idioms in English. A Corpus-based Approach*, Clarendon Press, Oxford.

New English Dictionary on Historical Principles, 1884–1928, edited by James A. H. Murray, H. Bradley, W. A. Craigie and C. T. Onions, Clarendon Press, Oxford.

New Oxford Dictionary of English, 2001, Oxford University Press, Oxford.

New Shorter Oxford English Dictionary on Historical Principles, 1993 (rev. edn), 2 vols, edited by Lesley Brown, Clarendon Press, Oxford.

Oakes, M., 1998, *Statistics for Corpus Linguistics*, Edinburgh University Press, Edinburgh.

Oxford Dictionary of New Words, 1997, edited by E. Knowles and J. Elliott, Oxford University Press, Oxford.

Oxford Dictionary of Sociology, 1998, edited by G. Marshall, Oxford University Press, Oxford.

Oxford–Duden German Dictionary German–English/English–German, 1999 (2nd edn), Oxford University Press, Oxford.

Oxford English Dictionary, 1989 (revised edition of the *New English Dictionary on Historical Principles*), 20 vols, prepared by J. A. Simpson and E. S. C. Weiner, Clarendon Press, Oxford.

Palmer, H. and A. S. Hornby, 1933, *The Second Interim Report on English Collocations*, Kaitakusha, Tokyo.

Pinker, S., 1994, *The Language Instinct: How the Mind Creates Language*, William Morrow, New York.

Putnam, H., 1975, The Meaning of 'Meaning', in *Mind, Language and Reality*, Philosophical Papers vol. 2.

Quirk, R., S. Greenbaum, G. Leech and J. Svartvik, 1985, *A Comprehensive Grammar of the English Language*, Longman, London.

Random House College Dictionary, 1975 (2nd edn), Random House, New York.

Renouf, Antoinette, 1987, 'Corpus development', in J.M. Sinclair (ed.), *Looking Up. An account of the COBUILD Project in Lexical computing*, HarperCollins, London, pp.1–22.

Robins, R. H., 1979 (2nd edn), *A Short History of Linguistics*, Longman, London.

Roget, Peter Mark, 1852, *Thesaurus of English Words and Phrases*, Longman, Brown, Green and Longman, London. (Various editions published later.)

Said, E. W., 1995, *Orientalism: Western Conceptions of the Orient*, Penguin, London.

Sampson, G., 1997, *Educating Eve: The 'Language Instinct' Debate*, Cassell, London.

de Saussure, Ferdinand, 1960, *Course in General Linguistics*, Peter Owen, London (translated by Wade Baskin).

de Saussure, Ferdinand, 1972, *Cours de Linguistique Générale*, Editions Payot, Paris (édition critique préparée par Tullio de Mauro).

de Saussure, Ferdinand, 1983, *Course in General Linguistics*, Duckworth, London (translated by Roy Harris).

Searle, J. R., 1983, *Intentionality: An Essay in the Philosophy of Mind*, Cambridge University Press, Cambridge.

Searle, J. R., 1992, *The Rediscovery of the Mind*, MIT Press, Cambridge, Massachusetts.

Searle, J. R., 1998, *Mind, Language and Reality*, Basic Books, New York.

Sinclair, J. (ed.), 1987, *Looking Up: An Account of the Cobuild Project in Lexical Computing*, HarperCollins, London.

Sinclair, J., 1991, *Corpus Collocation Concordance*, Oxford University Press, Oxford.

Sinclair, J., 1996, 'The Empty Lexicon', *International Journal of Corpus Linguistics* 1: 99–119.

Sinclair, J., 2003, *Reading Concordances*, Pearson Education, London.

Sinclair, J. (ed.), 2004, *How to Use Corpora in Language Teaching*, John Benjamins, Amsterdam

Sinclair, J. 2004, *Trust the Text. Language, Corpus and Discourse*, Routledge, London.

Sperber, D. and D. Wilson, 1998, The Mapping between the Mental and the Public Lexicon, in P. Carruthers and J. Boucher (eds), *Language and Thought*, Cambridge University Press, Cambridge.

Stubbs, M., 2001, *Words and Phrases: Corpus Studies of Lexical Semantics*, Blackwell Publishers, Oxford.

Svartvik, J. (ed.), 1990, *The London Corpus of Spoken English: Description and Research*, Lund Studies in English 82, Lund University Press, Lund.

Teubert, W., 2005, 'My version of corpus linguistics', *International Journal of Corpus Linguistics* 10(1), 1–13.

Tognini-Bonelli, E., 2001, *Corpus Linguistics at Work*, John Benjamins, Amsterdam.

Wierzbicka, A., 1996, *Semantics. Primes and Universals*, Oxford University Press, Oxford.

Wildhagen, K. and W. Héraucourt, 1963–72, *English–German/German–English Dictionary*, 2 vols, Brandstetter, Wiesbaden.

Corpora

The Bank of English, http://titania.bham.ac.uk/

British National Corpus, http://www.natcorp.ox.ac.uk/

Brown Corpus, manual available at http://icame.uib.no/brown/bcm.html

Czech National Corpus, http://ucnk.ff.cuni.cz/english/

IDS (Institut für Deutsche Sprache) corpus *COSMAS*, http://corpora.ids-mannheim.de/

International Corpus of English (ICE), http://www.ucl.ac.uk/english-usage/ice/

The Lancaster-Oslo/Bergen Corpus, manual available at http://khnt.hit.uib.no/icame/manuals/lob/INDEX.HTM

London Lund Corpus, http://khnt.hit.uib.no/icame/manuals/LONDLUND/INDEX.HTM

Språkbanken, http://spraakbanken.gu.se/

WordNet, http://www.cogsci.Princeton.edu/~wn/

Index

(words in bold can be found in the Glossary)